PCAT

THE OFFICIAL '80s PCAT PENCIL

PCAT

Preparation for the Pop-Culture Aptitude Test: Rad '80s Version

JOHN SELLERS

PCAT

Preparation for the Pop-Culture Aptitude Test:
Rad '80s Version

BACK BAY BOOKS

LITTLE, BROWN AND COMPANY

BOSTON   NEW YORK   TORONTO   LONDON

Photo credits appear on page 172.

ISBN 0-316-78068-5

10 9 8 7 6 5 4 3 2 1

another idea from becker&mayer!

Book design by Julia Sedykh.

Published simultaneously in Canada by Little, Brown & Company
(Canada) Limited
Printed in the United States of America

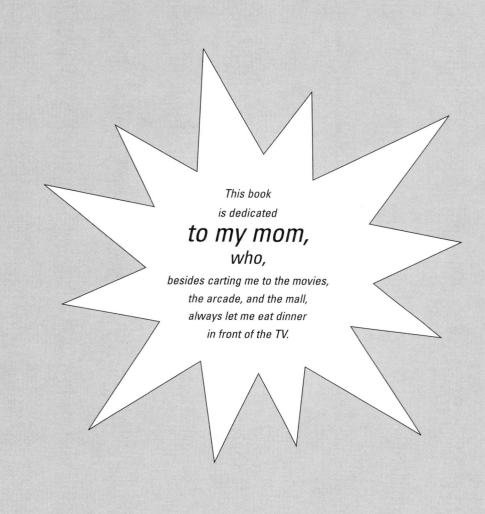

This book
is dedicated
to my mom,
who,
besides carting me to the movies,
the arcade, and the mall,
always let me eat dinner
in front of the TV.

Contents

Acknowledgments

A sincere "Thanks, dude" goes out to the people who helped make this book possible: Heidi von Schreiner, Geoff Kloske, Jennifer Worick, Jim Becker, and Andy Mayer.

Other fabulous prizes go out to these generous supporters: Karin Schulze, Philip Kim, Nicole "Klutz" Santistevan, Chris Bruno, Greg "Trial by Fire" Emmanuel, Bernie Su, Lydia Kang, my dad (who I once beat 105–12 in IntelliVision baseball), Mark Sellers, Matt Sellers, Matt "Inveraray" Larson, the entire 1993 *Michiganensian* staff, Jim Trout, everyone at *Time Out New York*, Jamie Bufalino, John Hodgman, Bob Kolker, Adam Sachs, Brett Martin, and Joel "Pleats" Stein.

Additionally, the author wishes to thank Aaron Buttrick, Greg Maynard, Tom Overly, Gordon Greer, Steve Seagly, and whoever came up with the idea for Donkey Kong.

Unless you were as stoned as Spicoli, you probably remember taking the SAT back in high school. What sober test-taker could ever forget filling in those tiny Scantron ovals with a No. 2 pencil, making very sure not to mark outside the lines? All of the hateful analogies, the vexing Venn diagrams, the intrusive STOP signs indicating the end of the sections — they mocked you in your dreams for weeks. When the test proctor barked, "Put down your pencils and close your booklets!" you were still a handful of questions shy of finishing the Verbal, dashing any hope Mom harbored of you getting into an Ivy League college.

But think about it. For all its gut-wrenching importance, that Saturday you spent taking the Scholastic Aptitude Test, or SAT, was just a huge waste of time. What, after all, did it really test? Your knowledge of algebra? Your ability to comprehend a passage about sunspots? Your mediocre score of 1100, though crippling your chance of going to Harvard, didn't even begin to gauge your real-world intelligence.

That's where the Pop-Culture Aptitude Test (PCAT) comes in. In the same way that the SAT quizzed you on the useless knowledge you had to learn in high school (like geometry), the PCAT tests the oodles of trivia that you've stored up since birth. It's the only standardized test that goes after the really important stuff, the stuff outside the realm of academia, the stuff that you use every day — *pop-culture stuff*.

The 1980s version of the PCAT is a good place to start. More than any other decade, the '80s are worth revisiting for their sheer entertainment value. When you think of some of the things that came from the decade — leg warmers, *Dynasty*, the Rubik's Cube, break dancing, Valley Girls — you'll realize that, besides being a tad embarrassing, it was a very memorable period in America's history. And hopefully, as you take the test on the following pages, you'll be happy to find that those days were, like, totally awesome, too.

So how much do you remember about the Big '80s? You'll probably do okay on the PCAT if at some point during the decade you did any of the following things: hung out with friends at a mall;

fed a dollar's worth of quarters into a Pac-Man machine; debated hard about buying a pair of parachute pants; spiked your hair with mousse; said the words "Gag me with a spoon"; plunged a straw into a Capri Sun fruit juice; or lip-synched to a tune by Corey Hart. If you did all of them, you just might score high enough to out-'80s all of your friends. Now that's something Mom could be proud of, even if you flubbed the SAT and didn't amount to very much.

So grab your No. 2 pencil, put on a Duran Duran CD, and get ready to relive the most radical decade ever — the 1980s.

PCAT

Preparation for the Pop-Culture Aptitude Test: Rad '80s Version

The Rad '80s

THE OFFICIAL '80s PCAT PENCIL

This first section of the PCAT is composed of eighty questions to get you in an '80s state of mind. Even though it's scored separately from the rest of the test (see "How to Figure Out Your Score," page 164), don't think that you can just skip it. That would be totally uncool.

Timeline matching

Directions: Below are four groups of five questions, each question consisting of a memorable '80s event (Column A) and a year (Column B). In each group, match the event in Column A with the year in Column B when it took place. If you get stuck, maybe it would help to thumb through some back issues of *USA Today* (debuted September 15, 1982). (Note: Each year in Column B will be chosen only once per group.)

A		B	
1.	John Hinckley shoots Ronald Reagan	(A)	1980
2.	John Lennon shot	(B)	1981
3.	AIDS virus identified	(C)	1982
4.	John Belushi OD's	(D)	1983
5.	United States invades Grenada	(E)	1984

A		B	
6.	"Black Monday" stock market crash	(A)	1985
7.	Chernobyl	(B)	1986
8.	Tiananmen Square massacre	(C)	1987
9.	New Coke introduced	(D)	1988
10.	"You're no Jack Kennedy"	(E)	1989

A		B	
11.	Sally Ride becomes first woman in space	(A)	1980
12.	Mount St. Helens erupts	(B)	1981
13.	Tylenol tainted with cyanide	(C)	1982
14.	Charles and Diana get married	(D)	1983
15.	Baby Fae implanted with baboon heart	(E)	1984

A		B	
16.	Rock Hudson admits that he has AIDS	(A)	1985
17.	Noriega indicted on drug bribery charges	(B)	1986
18.	*Exxon Valdez* runs aground	(C)	1987
19.	*Challenger* explodes	(D)	1988
20.	Baby Jessica falls down a well	(E)	1989

GO ON TO THE NEXT PAGE

Questions 21–28 refer to '80s slang.

Directions: Each question below consists of a word, phrase, or sentence from the '80s printed in capital letters, followed by five lettered words, phrases, or sentences. Choose the lettered answer that is *most similar* to the word, phrase, or sentence in capital letters.

21. DWEEB

    (A) airhead
    (B) ditz
    (C) geek
    (D) bimbo
    (E) space cadet

22. GNARLY

    (A) Psych!
    (B) Grody to the max.
    (C) Totally tubular!
    (D) This sucks, retard!
    (E) Word!

23. TAKE A CHILL PILL

    (A) Don't be such a spaz.
    (B) Bust a rhyme.
    (C) Do the nasty.
    (D) Just say no.
    (E) Eat my shorts.

24. THAT GUY IS BODACIOUS!

    (A) Look at that flamer!
    (B) Yon dude is bogue.
    (C) Barf-o-rama!
    (D) Omigod! What a studmuffin!
    (E) He's butt ugly!

25. TAKE OFF, HOSER

    (A) Go away, smart guy!
    (B) Shut your pie hole, scumbag!
    (C) Remove your clothing, dude.
    (D) Fly the plane, Lindbergh!
    (E) Fuck off, eh?

26. YOUR CAMARO IS BITCHIN'

    (A) Dude, your car is hellacious.
    (B) That thing sounds whack.
    (C) Your Camaro is beyond lame.
    (D) Your car is wicked, man.
    (E) You're in deep shit for buying that!

27. HE'S MAJORLY GROSS

    (A) He's fresh.
    (B) Gag me with a spoon!
    (C) That guy's queer.
    (D) The dude is totally righteous.
    (E) Fuckin' A! He's *bad!*

28. SMOOTH MOVE, EX-LAX

    (A) Totally rad, man.
    (B) You be illin'.
    (C) I'm shitting bricks!
    (D) Party on, dork!
    (E) That was lame, dude.

GO ON TO THE NEXT PAGE

Fill in the blanks

Directions: Each sentence below has one or two blanks, each blank indicating that something has been omitted. Beneath the sentence are five lettered items or sets of items. Choose the answer for each blank that best fits the meaning of the sentence as a whole.

Questions 29–38 refer to '80s fashion.

It was the best of times, it was the worst of times. It was the time of Ray•Bans, it was the time of leg warmers. It was the time for Reeboks, it was the time for parachute pants. Fill in the blanks about fab and not-so-fab '80s fashion.

29. If you wanted to, like, replicate the surfer look, you'd most probably be wearing ———— .

    (A) an Ocean Pacific T-shirt
    (B) Banana Republic
    (C) a Swatch
    (D) Guess? jeans
    (E) Lee Press-On Nails

30. In a memorable jeans commercial, Brooke Shields warned us that "Nothing comes between me and my ———— ."

    (A) Bonjours
    (B) Sassons
    (C) Chics
    (D) Calvins
    (E) Vanderbilts

31. The ultimate preppie would turn up the collar of his ———— shirt or put on ———— .

    (A) Polo; a Thriller jacket
    (B) Benetton; "three-day stubble"
    (C) Izod; an argyle sweater vest
    (D) "Frankie Says Relax"; a handful of jean-jacket buttons
    (E) zippered triangular-patterned; Bugle Boy jeans

32. ———— was a big salon request, while ———— were all the rage at the mall.

    (A) The wet look; Bermuda shorts
    (B) The Princess Di; plastic bracelets
    (C) Mousse; cardigans with untucked shirts
    (D) Feathered-back hair; "do rags"
    (E) All of the above

33. Corey Hart wore his ———— at night; *Moonlighting's* Cybill Shepherd was often photographed in ———— .

    (A) Izod; beef ads
    (B) Vuarnets; Air Jordans
    (C) Wayfarers; bowling shoes
    (D) Ray•Bans; Reeboks
    (E) parachute pants; Vans

34. If you were a dancer on *Fame* (or just craved that Jennifer Beals look), ———— were an essential element in your wardrobe; if you were Crockett on *Miami Vice*, then ———— were part of yours.

    (A) headbands; pastel socks
    (B) spandex pants; penny loafers
    (C) leg warmers; pastel T-shirts
    (D) ripped sweatshirts; paisley ties
    (E) all of the above

35. One of the Pet Shop Boys was almost always photographed wearing a ———— .

    (A) Boy cap
    (B) headband
    (C) Members Only jacket
    (D) skinny tie
    (E) hairpiece

GO ON TO THE NEXT PAGE

36. The mid-'80s '60s revival brought back —— ;
Bon Jovi influenced the —— look.

(A) the Twiggy look; Gap
(B) ponytails for men; ripped-jeans
(C) free love; big-hair
(D) clashing; yuppie
(E) guys' eyeliner; Jersey

37. If you wanted to be taunted by your peers, you
might wear —— or make sure you had a
—— on the back of your Polo shirt.

(A) floods; fag tag
(B) argyle sweaters; poop loop
(C) parachute pants; nerd alert
(D) Jams; smear of ketchup
(E) a Members Only jacket; KICK ME sign

38. Wearing an earring in —— was supposed
to mean that you were gay; wearing Armani
probably meant that you were —— .

(A) your nose; rich
(B) your navel; celibate
(C) both ears; cool
(D) your left ear; a preppie
(E) your right ear; a yuppie

Questions 39–43 refer to '80s video games.

Knowing all the patterns in Pac-Man was to the
'80s what knowing how to surf the web is to the
'90s. Ask any vidiot, though, and he'll give you a
token reply: you can get on-line in the privacy of
your own home, but there's no place like an arcade.

39. —— contained scenes entitled
"They Meet" and "The Chase."

(A) Popeye
(B) Donkey Kong
(C) Ms. Pac-Man
(D) Wizards of Wor
(E) Mario Bros.

40. The first laser disc game, —— , was about
Dirk the Daring's quest to save a hot princess.

(A) Cliffhanger
(B) Dragon's Lair
(C) Sinistar
(D) Dungeons & Dragons
(E) Space Ace

41. In —— , you used a trackball to ward off a
fierce attack; you had a ball on the track in
—— , which eventually ended up on
Saturday-morning TV.

(A) Moon Patrol; Track & Field
(B) Stargate; Q*Bert
(C) Missile Command; Pole Position
(D) Time Pilot; Bump 'N' Jump
(E) Space Invaders; Monaco G.P.

42. Flying around pterodactyls was a requisite of
—— ; avoiding flying scorpions was part of
the program in —— .

(A) Joust; Galaga
(B) Zookeeper; Centipede
(C) Defender; Asteroids
(D) Gladiator; Tempest
(E) Arkanoid; Dig Dug

43. You had to evade fireballs in —— , a game
based on a movie; in —— , which was
based on a band, you had to sidestep groupies.

(A) The Last Starfighter; The Grateful Dead
(B) Tron; Mötley Crüe
(C) Indiana Jones and the Temple of Doom;
The Cars
(D) Star Wars; Journey
(E) Star Trek; Duran Duran

GO ON TO THE NEXT PAGE

Video games logic

44. Given that you've just gobbled a power pellet in Pac-Man, and that you don't pass over any other dots in hot pursuit, how many points would you score if you ate all four blinking Ghost Monsters consecutively?

(A) 400
(B) 1,000
(C) 1,500
(D) 3,000
(E) 3,200

45. You want to play as much Frogger as you can, but your mom is coming to pick you up from Chuck E. Cheese in an hour and a half. Considering that it takes an average of 10 minutes to play a game, that you now have 12 tokens, and that you'll be grounded for a week if you make Mom wait, how many tokens will you still have when you leave the arcade?

(A) 0; a week's grounding is worth it for 12 games of Frogger.
(B) 2; you have time for 10 games, so you'll play 10 games.
(C) 3; you only have time for 9 games, and you know Mom.
(D) 12; a Frogger master hogged the game until Mom arrived.
(E) 12; you decided to watch Skee-Ball instead.

Which doesn't fit?

Directions: The following questions refer to '80s toys, technology, and trends. Each question below consists of something in capital letters, followed by five lettered answers. Choose the lettered answer that does *not* fit with the capitalized item.

46. FADS

(A) Lip-synching
(B) Lazer Tag
(C) break dancing
(D) the Hustle
(E) BABY ON BOARD signs

47. TRIVAL PURSUIT "PIE" COLORS

(A) green
(B) orange
(C) pink
(D) blue
(E) red

48. RUBIK'S CUBE SIDES

(A) black
(B) red
(C) white
(D) yellow
(E) orange

49. RUBIK'S PRODUCTS

(A) Chain
(B) Link
(C) Revenge
(D) Snake
(E) Triamid

50. PAC-MAN'S FOES

(A) Inky
(B) Blinky
(C) Pinky
(D) Moe
(E) Clyde

 **GO ON TO THE NEXT PAGE**

51. DOLLS

  (A) My Little Pony
  (B) Mister Mouth
  (C) My Buddy
  (D) Strawberry Shortcake
  (E) Cabbage Patch Kids

52. HOME GAME SYSTEMS

  (A) Atari 64
  (B) Commodore 64
  (C) IntelliVision
  (D) ColecoVision
  (E) Atari 3200

53. ROLE-PLAYING GAMES (RPGs)

  (A) Dungeons & Dragons
  (B) Twilight 2000
  (C) Zork
  (D) Gamma World
  (E) R.E.C.O.N.

54. DUNGEONS & DRAGONS

  (A) *Dungeon Master's Guide*
  (B) *Fiend Folio*
  (C) *Monster Manual*
  (D) *Player's Handbook*
  (E) *Adventurer's Survival Kit*

55. '80s INVENTIONS

  (A) video games
  (B) personal computers (PCs)
  (C) GameBoys
  (D) microwavable popcorn
  (E) Post-it Notes

'80s analogies

Directions: In each of the following questions, a related pair of names or shows is followed by five lettered pairs of names or shows. Select the lettered pair that best expresses a relationship similar to that expressed in the original pair.

Example:

Ronald Reagan : Nancy Reagan ::
  (A) Mikhail Gorbachev : Nadja Gorbachev
  (B) George Bush : Barbara Bush
  (C) Michael Jackson : Janet Jackson
  (D) Daryl Hall : John Oates
  (E) Michael Dukakis : Olympia Dukakis

Answer:

(B). Ronald and Nancy Reagan are married, as are George and Barbara Bush (although there's a rumor that Hall and Oates are also married).

Questions 56–62 refer to names in the news.

56. Magic Johnson : Pat Riley ::

  (A) Mike Tyson : Don King
  (B) Bo Jackson : Tommy Lasorda
  (C) Refrigerator Perry : Mike Ditka
  (D) Carl Lewis : Ronald Reagan
  (E) Larry Bird : Kevin McHale

57. Mary Lou Retton : Wheaties ::

  (A) Max Headroom : Dr Pepper
  (B) Michael Jordan : Reebok
  (C) Michael Jackson : New Coke
  (D) Grace Jones : Soloflex
  (E) Tip O'Neill : Hush Puppies

GO ON TO THE NEXT PAGE

58. Christie Brinkley : Billy Joel ::

   (A) Tatum O'Neal : Boris Becker
   (B) Milli : Vanilli
   (C) Paulina Porizkova : Rick Ocasek
   (D) Vanna White : Pat Sajak
   (E) Dr. Ruth Westheimer : Richard Simmons

59. Jackie Collins : *Hollywood Wives* ::

   (A) Stephen King : *Hellraiser*
   (B) Jay McInerney : *Slaves of New York*
   (C) Bill Cosby : *Fatherhood*
   (D) Danielle Steel : *The Stepford Wives*
   (E) Gallagher : *Why Smashing Watermelons Is Funny*

60. John Belushi : overdose ::

   (A) John Lennon : knife wound
   (B) Liberace : old age
   (C) Natalie Wood : stroke
   (D) Grace Kelly : hanging
   (E) Marvin Gaye : gunshot

61. Jim Bakker : embezzlement ::

   (A) Claus von Bülow : attempted murder
   (B) John DeLorean : vehicular manslaughter
   (C) Pete Rose : gun possession
   (D) Ivan Boesky : tax evasion
   (E) Oliver North : perjury

62. Sean Penn : Madonna ::

   (A) Eddie Van Halen : Valerie Bertinelli
   (B) Prince Charles : Lady Diana
   (C) Casey Kasem : Jean Kasem
   (D) Sylvester Stallone : Brigitte Nielsen
   (E) Michael Jackson : Bubbles the chimp

(Don't You) Forget About Me

Ten names you might not recall (but should):

The Australian Energizer dude — "Oy!"

J. J. Jackson — The low-voiced, Easy Reader–esque original MTV veejay

The Cavity Creeps — Crest Gel! Crest Gel! Crest Gel!

Clara Peller — "Where's the beef!"

Mead Trapper Keeper — A cool notebook in every locker

Yakov Smirnoff — The Russian "comedian" whose every joke began "In my country . . ."

Snuggles — If only he had been destuffed

Messy Marvin — Chocolate-syrup boy

Meeno Peluce — The greatest name an actor *(Best of the West, Voyagers!)* has ever had

Mr. Goodbody — The Barney of the '80s

GO ON TO THE NEXT PAGE

**Questions 63–70 ask you to identify
memorable '80s phenomena.**

Each question consists of a short statement followed by five lettered answers. Choose the one answer that is best described in the statement.

63. This workout guru sold the most videotapes.

(A) Jane Fonda
(B) Richard Simmons
(C) Body by Jake
(D) Mr. Goodbody
(E) Barney

64. This wedding attracted more TV viewers than any other.

(A) Luke and Laura's *General Hospital* wedding
(B) The Moonie wedding
(C) Lady Diana and Prince Charles's royal wedding
(D) Marcia and Jan Brady's double wedding
(E) Fergie and Prince Andrew's royal wedding

65. This person's nomination to the Supreme Court was nixed.

(A) A. Bartlett Giamatti
(B) Sandra Day O'Connor
(C) Thurgood Marshall
(D) Robert Bork
(E) C. Everett Koop

66. Prince mentioned this drug in "Sign 'O' the Times."

(A) crystal meth
(B) cocaine
(C) ecstasy
(D) heroin
(E) crack

67. This thing blew up in 1988.

(A) Mikey's head (from mixing Pop Rocks and Coke)
(B) The space shuttle *Challenger*
(C) Pan Am flight 103
(D) Mount St. Helens
(E) Chernobyl

68. He was Cyndi Lauper's professional wrestling partner.

(A) The Iron Sheik
(B) Captain Lou Albano
(C) Mr. T
(D) Randy "Macho Man" Savage
(E) Hulk Hogan

69. He wrote *Less Than Zero.*

(A) Hunter S. Thompson
(B) Bret Easton Ellis
(C) Tama Janowitz
(D) Stephen King
(E) Jay McInerney

70. His scandal involved Jessica Hahn.

(A) Jerry Falwell
(B) Rob Lowe
(C) Jimmy Swaggart
(D) Jim Bakker
(E) Gary Hart

GO ON TO THE NEXT PAGE

Ronald Reagan story problem

Directions: The following is a short biography of the fortieth President of the United States. After reading the passage, answer the ten questions that follow it.

When Ronald Reagan, the former actor and governor of California, soundly defeated Jimmy Carter in the 1980 presidential election, a new decade began in more ways than just the obvious. Although he was
[5] *shot a mere six months after being sworn in, the one-time* Bedtime for Bonzo *star survived to foster an environment that helped make the '80s what they were. Political correctness, yuppiedom, the Cold War, greed, and Jim Bakker all prospered during the*
[10] *Reagan years, and much of popular culture, from Madonna to Max Headroom, was influenced, for better or for worse, by the conservative policies of the Teflon President. Reagan's second wife, Nancy, who popularized a catchphrase, was thought by some to be*
[15] *secretly running the White House, but it was Ronald, not Nancy, who warded off a weak opponent in the 1984 election. Shortly thereafter, Reagan entered the hospital for cancer surgery. Once again, he survived, and after coming up with a crazy idea, served out his*
[20] *second term amid rumors that he was often asleep on the job. In 1989 George Bush moved into the White House, the Berlin Wall fell, and the Cold War ended. The '90s weren't far behind.*

71. John Hinckley, who tried to assassinate Reagan, was obsessed with ———— .

  (A) disco
  (B) Amy Carter
  (C) Bonzo the chimp
  (D) Nancy Reagan
  (E) Jodie Foster

72. Ronald Reagan's other films include all of the following EXCEPT ———— .

  (A) *Knute Rockne, All American*
  (B) *This Is the Army*
  (C) *Mr. Chips Goes to Washington*
  (D) *The Winning Team*
  (E) *Boy Meets Girl*

73. Reagan's first wife was a regular cast member of ———— .

  (A) *Dynasty*
  (B) *Punky Brewster*
  (C) *Dallas*
  (D) *Falcon Crest*
  (E) *Hotel*

74. Reagan's favorite '80s television program was ———— .

  (A) *Family Ties*
  (B) *Hail to the Chief*
  (C) *Max Headroom*
  (D) *Falcon Crest*
  (E) *Diff'rent Strokes*

75. Jim Bakker, referred to in line 9, was ———— .

  (A) sent to jail for having sex with a minor
  (B) killed in jail in 1989
  (C) kicked out of the Praise the Lord ministry for sexual discrimination
  (D) married to Tammy Faye Bakker, who was sent to jail on tax fraud charges
  (E) replaced as the president of the Praise the Lord ministry by Jerry Falwell

76. The phrase referred to in line 14 was ———— .

  (A) "Friends don't let friends drive drunk."
  (B) "Read my lips . . ."
  (C) "I don't recall."
  (D) "Just say no."
  (E) "This is your brain. . . . This is your brain on drugs. . . . Any questions?"

GO ON TO THE NEXT PAGE

77. The only state that the opponent referred to in line 16 won in the election was his home state of ———— .

   (A) Massachusetts
   (B) New Mexico
   (C) Texas
   (D) Minnesota
   (E) California

78. The type of cancer referred to in line 18 was that of the ———— .

   (A) lungs
   (B) colon
   (C) throat
   (D) skin
   (E) brain

79. The crazy idea referred to in line 19 was ———— .

   (A) "jellybeans for everyone"
   (B) Reaganomics
   (C) Glasnost
   (D) Star Wars defense system
   (E) Global Thermonuclear War

80. All of the following were major foes of Ronald Reagan EXCEPT ———— .

   (A) Mu'ammar al-Gadhafi
   (B) Mikhail Gorbachev
   (C) Saddam Hussein
   (D) Walter Mondale
   (E) Ayatollah Khomeini

STOP!

You have reached the end of Section I

Flicks

Directions: Each question or group of questions below is based on your knowledge of the Brat Pack. In answering some of the questions, it may be useful to draw a rough diagram or, at the very least, throw on the *Pretty in Pink* soundtrack. For each question, select the best answer.

Brat Pack logic

Questions 1–4

A wise casting director uses as many of seven Brat Pack actors — Molly Ringwald, Judd Nelson, Emilio Estevez, Ally Sheedy, Anthony Michael Hall, Demi Moore, and Andrew McCarthy — as she can. She is currently casting three movies (which are not shooting simultaneously): *Pretty in Pink, The Breakfast Club, and St. Elmo's Fire.* The seven Brat Packers above must be cast according to the following rules:

- If Ally Sheedy is in a film, then Emilio Estevez is in it, too.
- Demi Moore does not work with Anthony Michael Hall.
- If Molly Ringwald and Andrew McCarthy are in a movie together, then none of the other Brat Packers are.
- Each movie has at least two of the seven Brat Packers in it, but may have other actors in it.
- Judd Nelson always has a dumb look on his face.

1. Which of the following is an acceptable cast list for *Pretty in Pink* (a film about love transcending social strata)?

   (A) Molly Ringwald, Andrew McCarthy, Anthony Michael Hall
   (B) Demi Moore, Anthony Michael Hall, Judd Nelson
   (C) Ally Sheedy, Anthony Michael Hall, Andrew McCarthy
   (D) Molly Ringwald, Andrew McCarthy, Jon Cryer
   (E) Matthew Broderick, Mia Sara

GO ON TO THE NEXT PAGE

2. If Ally Sheedy and Anthony Michael Hall are in *The Breakfast Club* (a film about five high-school students stuck in Saturday detention), who *must* also be in it, too?

(A) Emilio Estevez
(B) Demi Moore
(C) Judd Nelson
(D) Molly Ringwald
(E) Andrew McCarthy

3. *St. Elmo's Fire*, a movie about postgraduation angst, stars five of the seven Brat Packers listed above. Given that Demi Moore and Andrew McCarthy are in the film, which two Brats were left out of this cultural touchstone?

(A) Emilio Estevez, Ally Sheedy
(B) Anthony Michael Hall, Molly Ringwald
(C) Judd Nelson, Molly Ringwald
(D) Ally Sheedy, Anthony Michael Hall
(E) Andrew McCarthy, Demi Moore

4. Which two Brat Packers will appear in only one of the three films?

(A) Judd Nelson, Ally Sheedy
(B) Andrew McCarthy, Demi Moore
(C) Demi Moore, Anthony Michael Hall
(D) Molly Ringwald, Ally Sheedy
(E) Emilio Estevez, Anthony Michael Hall

St. Elmo's Fire

GO ON TO THE NEXT PAGE

Brat Pack multiple choice

Questions 5–10 describe the Brat Packers' solo efforts.

It was inevitable, but stupid. Whenever a Brat left the comfy fold of the Pack, he or she would star in a movie that bombed at the box office. Choose the correct solo Brat Packer film from the five lettered answers.

5. Andrew McCarthy costars with Kim Cattrall in a movie with Jefferson Starship music.

(A) *Class*
(B) *Less Than Zero*
(C) *Mannequin*
(D) *Weekend at Bernie's*
(E) *Fresh Horses*

6. Ally Sheedy goes it alone as a rich girl put into a humbling situation by a fairy godmother.

(A) *St. Elmo's Fire*
(B) *Betsy's Wedding*
(C) *Oxford Blues*
(D) *Short Circuit*
(E) *Maid to Order*

7. Molly Ringwald bombs out in a 1988 film about teenage parenthood.

(A) *Betsy's Wedding*
(B) *King Lear*
(C) *P. K. and the Kid*
(D) *Fresh Horses*
(E) *For Keeps*

8. A hockey player (Rob Lowe) exorcises his personal demons to turn pro and exercises his good looks to tame an elusive small-town girl.

(A) *Youngblood*
(B) *Fresh Horses*
(C) *From the Hip*
(D) *Slap Shot*
(E) *About Last Night . . .*

9. Anthony Michael Hall picks up the wrong bag at the airport.

(A) *Something Wicked This Way Comes*
(B) *Out of Bounds*
(C) *Johnny Be Good*
(D) *That Was Then . . . This Is Now*
(E) *Blue City*

10. This 1985 road-trip movie stars Judd Nelson and non-Brat Kevin Costner.

(A) *Blue City*
(B) *One Crazy Summer*
(C) *Relentless*
(D) *Fandango*
(E) *Billionaire Boys Club*

The Breakfast Club

GO ON TO THE NEXT PAGE

Saturday Night Live matching

Questions 11–35 refer to *Saturday Night Live* alumni movies.

Saturday Night Live has produced more movie stars than any TV show in history, but that's not necessarily a good thing (see *It's Pat — the Movie* et al.). Much like the Brat Pack, there was generally safety in numbers; most solo movies by *SNL* alums usually tanked *(Dr. Detroit, Modern Problems)*. For the following questions, you are to look at the film and select:

(A) if Dan Aykroyd was in it
(B) if John Belushi was in it
(C) if Chevy Chase was in it
(D) if Bill Murray was in it
(E) if two or more of the above were in it

11. *The Blues Brothers*

12. *Stripes*

13. *Fletch*

14. *Ghostbusters*

15. *Caddyshack*

16. *Trading Places*

17. *Spies Like Us*

18. *¡Three Amigos!*

19. *Continental Divide*

20. *Under the Rainbow*

21. *The Great Outdoors*

22. *National Lampoon's Vacation*

23. *Neighbors*

24. *Deal of the Century*

25. *Caddyshack II*

A

B

C

D

GO ON TO THE NEXT PAGE

The next questions refer to
SNL: The Next Generation.

You are to look at the film and choose:

  (A) if Eddie Murphy was in it
  (B) if Billy Crystal was in it
  (C) if Christopher Guest was in it
  (D) if Martin Short was in it
  (E) if two or more of the above were in it

26. *When Harry Met Sally . . .*

27. *The Golden Child*

28. *Running Scared*

29. *Throw Momma from the Train*

30. *The Princess Bride*

31. *Best Defense*

32. *Innerspace*

33. *This Is Spinal Tap*

34. *Three Fugitives*

35. *Little Shop of Horrors*

Analogies

Directions: The following questions contain a pair of related items and the first part of a second pair of related items. Select the lettered answer that best expresses a relationship similar to that expressed in the original pair.

Questions 36–40 refer to
location, location, location.

36. Chicago : *Running Scared* :: Pittsburgh :

  (A) *Risky Business*
  (B) *Bright Lights, Big City*
  (C) *Down and Out in Beverly Hills*
  (D) *Flashdance*
  (E) *Less Than Zero*

37. New York : *Ghostbusters* :: London :

  (A) *A Fish Called Wanda*
  (B) *A Room with a View*
  (C) *Wall Street*
  (D) *Arthur*
  (E) *My Left Foot*

38. San Francisco : *48 HRS.* :: Detroit :

  (A) *Legal Eagles*
  (B) *Ferris Bueller's Day Off*
  (C) *Action Jackson*
  (D) *Gleaming the Cube*
  (E) *Poltergeist II: The Other Side*

GO ON TO THE NEXT PAGE

39. Los Angeles : *Die Hard* :: Washington, D.C. :

(A) *The Presidio*
(B) *Suspect*
(C) *No Mercy*
(D) *Little Nikita*
(E) *D.O.A.*

40. New Orleans : *The Big Easy* :: Cleveland :

(A) *The Outsiders*
(B) *The Natural*
(C) *Breathless*
(D) *Diner*
(E) *Howard the Duck*

**Questions 41–60 refer to
memorable roles.**

41. Axel Foley : Eddie Murphy :: Harry Crumb :

(A) Nick Nolte
(B) Jim Belushi
(C) Bill Murray
(D) John Candy
(E) Don Knotts

42. *The Elephant Man* : John Hurt :: *Mask* :

(A) Eric Stoltz
(B) Lou Diamond Phillips
(C) Sean Penn
(D) Sean Astin
(E) William Hurt

43. Michael J. Fox : Marty McFly :: Alan Ruck :

(A) Pony Boy
(B) Amadeus
(C) Cameron
(D) Booger
(E) Hans Gruber

44. Indiana Jones : Harrison Ford :: Buckaroo Banzai :

(A) Sigourney Weaver
(B) Bruce Willis
(C) Remo Williams
(D) Fred Ward
(E) Peter Weller

45. Dr. Peter Venkman : Bill Murray :: Dr. Raymond Stantz :

(A) Donald Pleasence
(B) Ernie Hudson
(C) Dan Aykroyd
(D) Harold Ramis
(E) Chevy Chase

GO ON TO THE NEXT PAGE

46. Ian Faith : *This Is Spiñal Tap* :: Large Marge :

   (A) *Uncle Buck*
   (B) *The Last American Virgin*
   (C) *Fatso*
   (D) *Pee-wee's Big Adventure*
   (E) *The Terminator*

47. Booger : *Revenge of the Nerds* :: Long Duk Dong :

   (A) *Revenge of the Nerds*
   (B) *Porky's*
   (C) *Sixteen Candles*
   (D) *Gung Ho*
   (E) *Action Jackson*

48. RoboCop : Peter Weller :: Freddy Krueger :

   (A) Robert Englund
   (B) Tim Curry
   (C) Peter MacNicol
   (D) Gordon Shumway
   (E) Mike Myers

49. Arnold Schwarzenegger : Conan the Barbarian :: Miles O'Keeffe :

   (A) the Beastmaster
   (B) the Earl of Greystoke
   (C) Conan the Destroyer
   (D) Tarzan, the Ape Man
   (E) Dragonslayer

50. *American Anthem* : Mitch Gaylord :: *Gymkata* :

   (A) Kurt Thomas
   (B) Brandon Lee
   (C) Jean-Claude Van Damme
   (D) Mitch Gaylord
   (E) Mary Lou Retton

51. Spicoli: *Fast Times at Ridgemont High* :: Grossberger :

   (A) *Bachelor Party*
   (B) *Meatballs 2*
   (C) *Platoon*
   (D) *Stripes*
   (E) *Stir Crazy*

52. The Karate Kid : Ralph Macchio :: Pony Boy :

   (A) Ralph Macchio
   (B) Tom Cruise
   (C) C. Thomas Howell
   (D) Henry Thomas
   (E) Rob Lowe

53. Jesus : Willem Dafoe :: John McClane :

   (A) Gil Gerard
   (B) Sylvester Stallone
   (C) Harrison Ford
   (D) Bruce Willis
   (E) Arnold Schwarzenegger

54. Shoeless Joe Jackson : Ray Liotta :: Crash Davis :

   (A) Kevin Costner
   (B) Robert Redford
   (C) Dennis Quaid
   (D) Mark Harmon
   (E) Burt Reynolds

55. Bishop : *Aliens* :: Lobot :

   (A) *The Empire Strikes Back*
   (B) *Octopussy*
   (C) *Short Circuit*
   (D) *D.A.R.Y.L.*
   (E) *Cyborg*

56. Clark Griswold : Chevy Chase :: Leo Getz :

   (A) Bronson Pinchot
   (B) Joe Pesci
   (C) Bob Hoskins
   (D) Jim Carrey
   (E) Joe Piscopo

GO ON TO THE NEXT PAGE

57. The Keymaster : *Ghostbusters* :: Argyle :

    (A) *Ghostbusters II*
    (B) *To Live and Die in L.A.*
    (C) *Die Hard*
    (D) *Who's That Girl?*
    (E) *Moving Violations*

58. The Regulators : *Young Guns* :: the Wolverines :

    (A) *Band of the Hand*
    (B) *Red Dawn*
    (C) *The Karate Kid*
    (D) *Streets of Fire*
    (E) *Solarbabies*

59. Sophie Zawistowska : Meryl Streep :: Alex Forrest :

    (A) Meryl Streep
    (B) Geena Davis
    (C) Glenn Close
    (D) Goldie Hawn
    (E) Cher

60. Michael Keaton : Batman :: Sam J. Jones :

    (A) Zorro
    (B) Captain America
    (C) The Flash
    (D) Buck Rogers
    (E) Flash Gordon

Name the film

Directions: The next twenty questions contain a list of four actors followed by five lettered films. Choose the one movie in which all the actors appear.

61. Kevin Bacon, Christopher Penn, Dianne Wiest, Sarah Jessica Parker

    (A) *Friday the 13th*
    (B) *Quicksilver*
    (C) *Footloose*
    (D) *All the Right Moves*
    (E) *Planes, Trains and Automobiles*

62. Phoebe Cates, Nicolas Cage, Eric Stoltz, Forest Whitaker

    (A) *Private School*
    (B) *Fast Times at Ridgemont High*
    (C) *Gremlins*
    (D) *Valley Girl*
    (E) *Platoon*

63. Jami Gertz, John Cusack, Joan Cusack, Gedde Watanabe

    (A) *Volunteers*
    (B) *The Karate Kid*
    (C) *Gung Ho*
    (D) *The Sure Thing*
    (E) *Sixteen Candles*

64. Tim Robbins, Tom Skerritt, Meg Ryan, Anthony Edwards

    (A) *Bull Durham*
    (B) *Gotcha!*
    (C) *Stealing Home*
    (D) *Top Gun*
    (E) *D.O.A.*

GO ON TO THE NEXT PAGE

65. Dianne Wiest, Mary Steenburgen, Joaquin Phoenix, Martha Plimpton

(A) *Ragtime*
(B) *Back to the Future, Part II*
(C) *Miss Firecracker*
(D) *Parenthood*
(E) *A Midsummer Night's Sex Comedy*

66. Paul Reubens, Ray Charles, Carrie Fisher, John Candy

(A) *Big Top Pee-wee*
(B) *Under the Rainbow*
(C) *Spaceballs*
(D) *Amazon Women on the Moon*
(E) *The Blues Brothers*

67. Geena Davis, Dabney Coleman, Bill Murray, Teri Garr

(A) *The Razor's Edge*
(B) *The Fly*
(C) *Tootsie*
(D) *Mr. Mom*
(E) *Fletch*

68. Kevin Costner, JoBeth Williams, Meg Tilly, Jeff Goldblum

(A) *Poltergeist II: The Other Side*
(B) *Sizzle Beach, U.S.A.*
(C) *Earth Girls Are Easy*
(D) *The Big Chill*
(E) *Transylvania 6–5000*

Porky's

Ten totally '80s movie titles

Breakin' 2: Electric Boogaloo (1984)

Reform School Girls (1986)

Red Dawn (1984)

Hardbodies 2 (1986)

Turk 182! (1985)

My Dinner with Andrè (1981)

Porky's (1981)

Ladyhawke (1985)

C.H.U.D. [Cannibalistic Humanoid Underground Dwellers] (1984)

C.H.U.D. II — Bud the Chud (1989)

GO ON TO THE NEXT PAGE

69. Tim Robbins, Mickey Rooney, Eartha Kitt, Terry Jones

    (A) *Erik the Viking*
    (B) *Time Bandits*
    (C) *The Black Stallion Returns*
    (D) *Senior Trip*
    (E) *Monty Python's The Meaning of Life*

70. Jerry Stiller, Pia Zadora, Ric Ocasek, Deborah Harry

    (A) *Sid & Nancy*
    (B) *Troop Beverly Hills*
    (C) *The Adventures of Baron Munchausen*
    (D) *This Is Spinal Tap*
    (E) *Hairspray*

71. Joan Allen, Jim Carrey, Helen Hunt, Nicolas Cage

    (A) *Earth Girls Are Easy*
    (B) *Pink Cadillac*
    (C) *Once Bitten*
    (D) *Club Paradise*
    (E) *Peggy Sue Got Married*

72. Elizabeth Peña, Tracy Nelson, Little Richard, Bette Midler

    (A) *Outrageous Fortune*
    (B) *Beaches*
    (C) *Down and Out in Beverly Hills*
    (D) *Ruthless People*
    (E) *Stella*

73. Yakov Smirnoff, Jamie Lee Curtis, Jeff Goldblum, John Lithgow

    (A) *A Fish Called Wanda*
    (B) *The Adventures of Buckaroo Banzai Across the Eighth Dimension*
    (C) *Moscow on the Hudson*
    (D) *Heartburn*
    (E) *Twilight Zone—The Movie*

74. Daniel Day-Lewis, Martin Sheen, John Gielgud, Candice Bergen

    (A) *My Left Foot*
    (B) *Gandhi*
    (C) *A Room with a View*
    (D) *Arthur*
    (E) *Brideshead Revisited*

75. Max von Sydow, Linda Hunt, Dean Stockwell, Sean Young

    (A) *Blade Runner*
    (B) *The Year of Living Dangerously*
    (C) *Dreamscape*
    (D) *Dune*
    (E) *Blue Velvet*

76. Nora Dunn, Ricki Lake, Alec Baldwin, Joan Cusack

    (A) *Working Girl*
    (B) *She's Having a Baby*
    (C) *Broadcast News*
    (D) *Hairspray*
    (E) *Beetlejuice*

77. Robert Downey, Jr., Dennis Hopper, Danny Aiello, Harvey Keitel

    (A) *Rumble Fish*
    (B) *Less Than Zero*
    (C) *1969*
    (D) *The Pick-Up Artist*
    (E) *Chances Are*

78. Billy Dee Williams, Jack Palance, Robert Wuhl, Kim Basinger

    (A) *9½ Weeks*
    (B) *The Natural*
    (C) *Batman*
    (D) *Never Say Never Again*
    (E) *My Stepmother Is an Alien*

GO ON TO THE NEXT PAGE

79. Liam Neeson, Daniel Day-Lewis, Laurence Olivier, Mel Gibson

    (A) *The Bounty*
    (B) *Hamlet*
    (C) *Lethal Weapon*
    (D) *Gallipoli*
    (E) *The Year of Living Dangerously*

80. Joe Flaherty, Flea, Billy Zane, Elisabeth Shue

    (A) *Link*
    (B) *Back to the Future, Part II*
    (C) *Cocktail*
    (D) *Adventures in Babysitting*
    (E) *The Karate Kid*

Name the actor

Directions: Each question below contains a list of four films followed by five lettered actors. Choose the one actor that has been in all four films.

81. *Endless Love, The Outsiders, Taps, Legend*

    (A) Matt Dillon
    (B) Emilio Estevez
    (C) Ralph Macchio
    (D) Tom Cruise
    (E) Ricky Schroder

82. *The January Man, Compromising Positions, The Hunger, The Witches of Eastwick*

    (A) Glenn Close
    (B) Kevin Kline
    (C) Susan Sarandon
    (D) Meryl Streep
    (E) Cher

83. *Salvador, About Last Night . . . , The Man With One Red Shoe, K-9*

    (A) Andrew McCarthy
    (B) Jim Belushi
    (C) Tom Hanks
    (D) Willem Dafoe
    (E) James Woods

84. *The Outsiders, Red Dawn, Youngblood, Road House*

    (A) Kelly Lynch
    (B) Rob Lowe
    (C) Patrick Swayze
    (D) Charlie Sheen
    (E) C. Thomas Howell

GO ON TO THE NEXT PAGE

85. *Altered States, Children of a Lesser God, Broadcast News, The Big Chill*

   (A) Marlee Matlin
   (B) William Hurt
   (C) Albert Brooks
   (D) Kevin Costner
   (E) Meg Tilly

86. *Tin Men; This Is Spinal Tap; Good Morning, Vietnam; When Harry Met Sally . . .*

   (A) Billy Crystal
   (B) Dana Carvey
   (C) Danny DeVito
   (D) Christopher Guest
   (E) Bruno Kirby

87. *Something Wild, Heartburn, Radio Days, Terms of Endearment*

   (A) Jeff Goldblum
   (B) Melanie Griffith
   (C) Ann Magnuson
   (D) Jeff Daniels
   (E) Jack Nicholson

88. *The Morning After, Against All Odds, The Jagged Edge, Tron*

   (A) Jeff Bridges
   (B) Karen Allen
   (C) Phil Collins
   (D) Beau Bridges
   (E) Bruce Boxleitner

Five people **who should never have been** *allowed to act*

Cyndi Lauper

Corey Haim

Marc Singer

Andrew McCarthy

Yahoo Serious

GO ON TO THE NEXT PAGE

89. *The Sure Thing, Revenge of the Nerds, Top Gun, Gotcha!*

    (A) Curtis Armstrong
    (B) John Cusack
    (C) Joan Cusack
    (D) Anthony Edwards
    (E) Nicolas Cage

90. *Broadcast News, The Journey of Natty Gann, Class, Stand By Me*

    (A) River Phoenix
    (B) Wil Wheaton
    (C) John Cusack
    (D) Kiefer Sutherland
    (E) Richard Dreyfuss

91. *Dream a Little Dream, License to Drive, The Lost Boys, The Goonies*

    (A) Kiefer Sutherland
    (B) Corey Haim
    (C) Corey Feldman
    (D) Sean Astin
    (E) Jami Gertz

92. *Babes in Toyland, Youngblood, Parenthood, Dangerous Liaisons*

    (A) Michelle Pfeiffer
    (B) Joaquin Phoenix
    (C) Uma Thurman
    (D) John Malkovich
    (E) Keanu Reeves

93. *Fast Times at Ridgemont High, The Wild Life, Say Anything . . . , Some Kind of Wonderful*

    (A) Mary Stuart Masterson
    (B) Sean Penn
    (C) Christopher Penn
    (D) Nicolas Cage
    (E) Eric Stoltz

94. *One Crazy Summer, Blame It on Rio, We're No Angels, Wisdom*

    (A) John Cusack
    (B) Demi Moore
    (C) Sean Penn
    (D) Emilio Estevez
    (E) Michael Caine

95. *Howard the Duck, Top Gun, Fraternity Vacation, Erik the Viking*

    (A) Lea Thompson
    (B) Meg Ryan
    (C) Tom Berenger
    (D) Tim Robbins
    (E) Mimi Rogers

96. *Gremlins, Beverly Hills Cop II, Ruthless People, Stripes*

    (A) Bronson Pinchot
    (B) Judge Reinhold
    (C) Harold Ramis
    (D) Paul Reiser
    (E) Bill Pullman

97. *Endless Love, Crossroads, The Lost Boys, Solarbabies*

    (A) Jami Gertz
    (B) James Spader
    (C) Brooke Shields
    (D) Ralph Macchio
    (E) Jason Patric

98. *Conan the Barbarian, Allan Quartermain and the Lost City of Gold, Soul Man, Three Fugitives*

    (A) Rae Dawn Chong
    (B) Brigitte Nielsen
    (C) Grace Jones
    (D) Alan Ruck
    (E) James Earl Jones

GO ON TO THE NEXT PAGE

99. *Max Dugan Returns; At Close Range; 1969; Bright Lights, Big City*

    (A) Cheech Marin
    (B) Dennis Hopper
    (C) Donald Sutherland
    (D) Crispin Glover
    (E) Kiefer Sutherland

100. *Action Jackson, Police Academy 4: Citizens on Patrol, King Solomon's Mines, Allan Quartermain and the Lost City of Gold*

    (A) Carl Weathers
    (B) Richard Chamberlain
    (C) Sharon Stone
    (D) Steve Guttenberg
    (E) Vanity

A few Guttenberg questions

Questions 101–107 refer to the following passage:

After starring in the strange, strange Can't Stop the Music *(alongside the Village People and Bruce Jenner),* **Steve Guttenberg,** *the most unlikely super-star of the '80s, landed a role in one of the best "guy"*
[5] *movies of all time. (That 1982 ensemble film also starred an actor who later went on to the inexplicably popular '90s TV show* Wings.) *Then in 1984 Guttenberg appeared in the first installment of what became a seemingly endless series of slapstick films.*
[10] *But Guttenberg's breakthrough year was 1985, when he starred in the feel-good movie* Cocoon; *that role led to a film about a clever robot the following year, and even more success in 1987. In that fateful year, Guttenberg was in* five *movies — most notably*
[15] *the one in which he used the word "doodle" to refer to going "number two." Since then, however, his career has been pretty much in the crapper.*

Steve Guttenberg

GO ON TO THE NEXT PAGE

101. The movie referred to in lines 4–5 is ——— .

    (A) *The Big Chill*
    (B) *Diner*
    (C) *Planes, Trains and Automobiles*
    (D) *Spies Like Us*
    (E) *Police Academy*

102. That movie also starred all of the following EXCEPT ——— .

    (A) Mickey Rourke
    (B) Kevin Bacon
    (C) Ellen Barkin
    (D) Daniel Stern
    (E) JoBeth Williams

103. The actor referred to in line 6 ——— .

    (A) is the brother of the woman who played TV's Wonder Woman
    (B) played a character named Georgi Orlav
    (C) is the brother of the woman who played TV's Mary Beth Lacey
    (D) is none other than Paul Reiser
    (E) is none other than Steven Weber

104. The movie referred to in lines 8–9 is ——— .

    (A) the first of two *Airplane!* movies
    (B) the first *Lethal Weapon* movie
    (C) the first of nine *Friday the 13th* movies
    (D) the first of seven *Police Academy* movies
    (E) the first of five *Nightmare on Elm Street* movies

105. The movie about the robot in line 12 ——— .

    (A) had a sequel in 1988 starring Fisher Stevens
    (B) was directed by Ron Howard
    (C) costarred Andie MacDowell
    (D) won an Academy Award for best special effects
    (E) was called *WarGames*

106. In the 1987 movie referred to in line 15 ——— .

    (A) Guttenberg plays a computer nerd
    (B) a boy who was rumored to have hanged himself can be seen behind a curtain in one scene
    (C) Ted Danson plays a struggling actor
    (D) three bachelors take care of a little baby boy
    (E) Tom Selleck has a nude scene

107. The other four 1987 movies Guttenberg starred in include all of the following EXCEPT ——— .

    (A) *Surrender*
    (B) *Cocoon: The Return*
    (C) *The Bedroom Window*
    (D) *Police Academy 4: Citizens on Patrol*
    (E) *Amazon Women on the Moon*

GO ON TO THE NEXT PAGE

Matthew Broderick logic

Questions 108–115 refer to the following passage, culled from the syllabus for a class at Smith State Community College:

Acting 101 — Legends

*This semester we will focus on the best actor of the 1980s — **Matthew Broderick.** Over the next few*
[5] *months, this course will walk you through the oeuvre of the great boyish actor, who, by consistently choosing quality roles, finished the decade miles ahead of his peers. From his auspicious 1983 debut in a Neil Simon movie to the sprawling Civil War*
[10] *drama* Glory *in 1989, Broderick landed parts that were moving or important, or both. We'll discuss the movie in which he starred opposite Ally Sheedy and a computer. We'll then turn our focus to his most memorable role, Ferris Bueller, and explore the many*
[15] *talents that Broderick exhibited therein. We'll even take in* Ladyhawke, *a rare Broderick misfire, as it provides interesting insight into why actors choose the roles they do. Other movies studied include* Project X *and* Family Business. *Reenactments for course credit.*
[20] *(Next semester's topic:* **Rae Dawn Chong***)*

108. The Neil Simon film mentioned in lines 8–9 is ——— .

    (A) *Biloxi Blues*
    (B) *Brighton Beach Memoirs*
    (C) *Max Dugan Returns*
    (D) *Torch Song Trilogy*
    (E) *I Ought to Be in Pictures*

109. The computer referred to in lines 11–13 was given by its creator the name of ——— .

    (A) DefCon 3
    (B) Hal
    (C) WHOMPP
    (D) NORAD
    (E) Joshua

110. Broderick's character challenges this computer to a game of ——— .

    (A) chess
    (B) Global Thermonuclear War
    (C) Stratego
    (D) WarGames
    (E) DefCon 1

111. The "many talents" that Broderick exhibits in *Ferris Bueller's Day Off*, referred to in lines 13–15, include all of the following EXCEPT ——— .

    (A) impersonating Richard Nixon
    (B) driving a Ferrari no-handed
    (C) catching a foul ball at a Chicago Cubs game
    (D) making out with Mia Sara
    (E) lip-synching a Beatles song at a parade

GO ON TO THE NEXT PAGE

112. Broderick's costar in *Ladyhawke* is ——— .

(A) Sean Connery
(B) Mia Sara
(C) Sharon Stone
(D) Michelle Pfeiffer
(E) Patrick Dempsey

113. *Project X* is a movie about ——— .

(A) a homemade nuclear bomb
(B) chimpanzees
(C) a high-school science experiment
(D) extraterrestrials
(E) life at a tenement building in Lower Manhattan

114. *Family Business* costars none of the following EXCEPT ——— .

(A) Bruno Kirby
(B) Jason Robards, Jr.
(C) Robert Redford
(D) Marlon Brando
(E) Sean Connery

115. If you took this class, you might also learn that Broderick ——— .

(A) won an Oscar for his role in *Glory*
(B) started his career on *General Hospital*
(C) is the nephew of *Hotel*'s James Brolin
(D) accidentally killed a few people in Northern Ireland in 1987
(E) ran the New York Marathon in 1988 and came in 2043rd

GO ON TO THE NEXT PAGE

Action movie quote ID

Directions: Each question below contains a scene from an '80s action movie followed by five lettered quotes. From these, select the quote that is the next line in the movie.

116. Mr. Miyagi is giving his pupil a hard time during karate training. For reasons unbeknownst to the student, Miyagi makes him detail a car. How does Miyagi instruct the kid to do it?

   (A) "Buff this."
   (B) "Don't forget to wax it."
   (C) "Show me Paint the Fence."
   (D) "Wax on, wax off."
   (E) "Cars don't hit back."

117. The caped crusader scares the wits out of a burglar. Before getting pulverized, the thief asks, "Who are you?" What does Michael Keaton say?

   (A) "Your worst nightmare."
   (B) "What's it to you, punk?"
   (C) "I'm Batman."
   (D) "I'm faster than a rolling O."
   (E) "I'm the Pied Piper of Hamlin, creep."

118. In *Poltergeist,* the blond daughter of Craig T. Nelson and JoBeth Williams is watching a snow-filled television set. She says . . .

   (A) "They're baaack!"
   (B) "They're coming!"
   (C) "Where's Fat Albert?"
   (D) █want my MTV."
   (E) "They're heeeere!"

119. In *Sudden Impact,* a man is holding a gun to the head of a hostage, and Dirty Harry is aiming his massive gun at the man. What does Dirty Harry say?

   (A) "Meet Smith and Wesson."

   (B) "Go ahead, make my day."
   (C) "What'll it be, punk?"
   (D) "You got two choices, kid: live or die."
   (E) "Mine's bigger."

120. The Terminator enters a police station and asks for prisoner Sarah Connor. When the desk clerk tells him that he can't see her, what does the Arnold say?

   (A) "Aw, schucks!"
   (B) "I will be back soon."
   (C) "You'll be sorry."
   (D) "Large Marge sent me."
   (E) "I'll be back."

121. Ivan Drago meets Rocky in the ring for the first time. How does the Soviet greet our hero?

   (A) "America sucks."
   (B) "I'm going to bust you like a melon."
   (C) "I had fun with Adrian last night."
   (D) "I must break you."
   (E) "Prepare to die."

122. In *The Empire Strikes Back,* Luke Skywalker must learn how to be a Jedi from the wizened Muppet Yoda. Before he begins the training, Luke says, "I'm not afraid." What does Yoda reply?

   (A) "You will be."
   (B) "You the man!"
   (C) "The Force is strong in your family."
   (D) "Good. Your training is almost complete."
   (E) "That is why you fail."

123. When Clubber Lang is asked for his prediction of his upcoming fight with the Italian Stallion, Rocky Balboa, what is his reply?

   (A) "Don't bet against me."
   (B) "It's gonna be a close one."
   (C) "Me in three."
   (D) "I pity the fool."
   (E) "Pain."

GO ON TO THE NEXT PAGE

124. Indiana Jones picks up a piece of fruit from a bowl on a table while talking to his friend Sallah. When he throws the fruit up in the air to catch it in his mouth, Sallah snatches it from the air. What does Sallah say?

(A) "You'll get nothing and like it!"
(B) "Poison!"
(C) "Wait! Look at the monkey!"
(D) "Taste bad."
(E) "Bad dates."

125. In *RoboCop*, the bad guys are sitting around their hideout plotting evil things and watching a television show with lots of scantily clad females. What does the guy on the television show say?

(A) "I like it!"
(B) "Baby got back!"
(C) "I'd buy that for a dollar!"
(D) "She's stacked!"
(E) "Come to papa."

Sylvester Stallone vs. Arnold Schwarzenegger
Who Won?

In an *Over the Top* arm wrestling contest, a Stallone-Schwarzenegger matchup would be pretty much a dead heat. Here are other ways to see which muscle man is stronger:

Category	Sylvester Stallone	Arnold Schwarzenegger	Winner
Big movie	*Rocky III*	*Conan the Barbarian*	Sly
Military movie	*Rambo*	*Commando*	Sly
Bad movie	*Cobra*	*Raw Deal*	pick 'em
Notable costar	Mr. T	Jesse "the Body" Ventura	Sly
Buddy flick	*Tango and Cash*	*Red Heat*	Arnold
Best acting	*First Blood*	*The Terminator*	Arnold
Comedy	*Rhinestone*	*Twins*	Arnold
Famous flame	Brigitte Nielsen	Maria Shriver	Sly
Famous relative	Frank Stallone	none	Arnold
Intelligibility	slurring	Austrian	pick 'em
Tiebreaker:			
More letters	17	20	Arnold

Arnold
wins!

GO ON TO THE NEXT PAGE

Comedy movie quote ID

Questions 126–145 refer to '80s comedies.

Here, just the quote is given, followed by five lettered movie titles. Choose the comedy that the line came from.

126. "He slimed me."

 (A) *Repo Man*
 (B) *Ghostbusters*
 (C) *Poltergeist*
 (D) *Leonard Part 6*
 (E) *Ghostbusters II*

127. "Give me a keg of beer."

 (A) *Back to the Future*
 (B) *Three O'Clock High*
 (C) *Teen Wolf*
 (D) *Ferris Bueller's Day Off*
 (E) *Can't Buy Me Love*

128. "You'll get nothing and like it!"

 (A) *Biloxi Blues*
 (B) *Bull Durham*
 (C) *Caddyshack*
 (D) *Neighbors*
 (E) *48 HRS.*

129. "Orange whip? Orange whip? Three orange whips, please."

 (A) *Fatso*
 (B) *Beverly Hills Cop II*
 (C) *The Blues Brothers*
 (D) *The Stuff*
 (E) *Delivery Boys*

130. "Baby fishmouth! Baby fishmouth!"

 (A) *One Crazy Summer*
 (B) *Valley Girl*
 (C) *Ferris Bueller's Day Off*
 (D) *Ice Pirates*
 (E) *When Harry Met Sally . . .*

131. "Does this proposition entail me dressing up like Little Bo Peep?"

 (A) *Bachelor Party*
 (B) *Fletch*
 (C) *Who's Harry Crumb?*
 (D) *Spies Like Us*
 (E) *Police Academy*

132. "I can't believe I gave my panties to a geek."

 (A) *Back to School*
 (B) *Spring Break*
 (C) *Fast Times at Ridgemont High*
 (D) *Sixteen Candles*
 (E) *Hot Dog . . . the Movie!*

133. "I'll be taking this box of Huggies, and whatever cash you got."

 (A) *Three Fugitives*
 (B) *Baby Boom*
 (C) *Raising Arizona*
 (D) *The Golden Child*
 (E) *Uncle Buck*

134. "Beef jerky! Beef jerky time!"

 (A) *Eating Raoul*
 (B) *Big*
 (C) *Trading Places*
 (D) *The Golden Child*
 (E) *Moscow on the Hudson*

GO ON TO THE NEXT PAGE

135. "Lighten up, Francis."

    (A) *City Heat*
    (B) *Stand by Me*
    (C) *Back to the Future*
    (D) *Cheech and Chong's The Corsican Brothers*
    (E) *Stripes*

136. " 'At's not a knife. 'At's a knife."

    (A) *"Crocodile" Dundee*
    (B) *Commando*
    (C) *The Golden Child*
    (D) *Spies Like Us*
    (E) *The Principal*

137. "I've got two words for you: Shut the fuck up!"

    (A) *Risky Business*
    (B) *48 HRS.*
    (C) *Midnight Run*
    (D) *Fletch*
    (E) *Running Scared*

138. "He's doing the African Anteater Dance."

    (A) *Can't Buy Me Love*
    (B) *Dirty Dancing*
    (C) *Breakin' 2: Electric Boogaloo*
    (D) *Bachelor Party*
    (E) *The Gods Must Be Crazy*

139. "To call you stupid would be an insult to stupid people."

    (A) *Stir Crazy*
    (B) *Midnight Run*
    (C) *Fletch Lives*
    (D) *A Fish Called Wanda*
    (E) *Skin Deep*

140. "Ruprecht, were you banging on your pots again?"

    (A) *Dirty Rotten Scoundrels*
    (B) *Disorderlies*
    (C) *Modern Problems*
    (D) *D.C. Cab*
    (E) *Coming to America*

141. "Mom, Dad — don't touch it! It's evil!"

    (A) *Better Off Dead*
    (B) *Time Bandits*
    (C) *Adventures in Babysitting*
    (D) *The Toxic Avenger*
    (E) *The Goonies*

142. "No one laughs at a master of quack-foo."

    (A) *Bugs Bunny's 3rd Movie: 1001 Rabbit Tales*
    (B) *Howard the Duck*
    (C) *Police Academy 2: Their First Assignment*
    (D) *Who Framed Roger Rabbit*
    (E) *Going Berserk*

143. "Laugh while you can, monkey boy!"

    (A) *The Adventures of Buckaroo Bonzai Across the Eighth Dimension*
    (B) *Harry and the Hendersons*
    (C) *Revenge of the Nerds*
    (D) *The Sure Thing*
    (E) *Pee-wee's Big Adventure*

GO ON TO THE NEXT PAGE

144. "Take this quarter, go downtown, and have a rat gnaw that thing off your face."

   (A) *Best Defense*
   (B) *Neighbors*
   (C) *Caddyshack*
   (D) *Uncle Buck*
   (E) *Big Top Pee-wee*

145. "Now what are my genitals supposed to do?"

   (A) *Fraternity Vacation*
   (B) *National Lampoon's Class Reunion*
   (C) *Bachelor Party*
   (D) *Fast Times at Ridgemont High*
   (E) *Blind Date*

Freddy Krueger vs. *Jason*
Who Won?

They both killed a lot of teenagers in their many, many movies, but in a head-to-head slashfest, which bruiser would win?

Category	Freddy Krueger	Jason	Winner
Terror zone	Elm Street	Camp Crystal Lake	Freddy
Costume	Striped sweater	Goalie mask	Jason
Preferred weapon	razor-sharp appendages	machete	Freddy
Amount of blood	some	scads	Jason
Number of sequels	5	8	pick 'em
Soundtrack cut	"Dream Warriors"	———	pick 'em
Stalking music	none	ch-ch-ch-ch-ch	Jason
Mute?	nope	yep	Freddy
Tiebreaker:			
Notable victim	Johnny Depp	Kevin Bacon	Freddy

Freddy
wins!

GO ON TO THE NEXT PAGE

Godlike directors

Directions: They were the greatest filmmakers of the decade. Looking at the world from totally different perspectives, John Hughes and Steven Spielberg generated one hit after another in the '80s. As their movies best represent the decade, you shouldn't need much information to identify them.

Questions 146–155 below consist of a description of a scene in a John Hughes film, followed by five lettered movies.

Choose the movie that best fits the description.

146. A vice principal tells a mother that her son has been absent from school "*nine times.*"

(A) *Pretty in Pink*
(B) *The Breakfast Club*
(C) *Fast Times at Ridgemont High*
(D) *A Night in the Life of Jimmy Reardon*
(E) *Ferris Bueller's Day Off*

147. Someone says, "Blaine? His name is Blaine? That's a major appliance, that's not a name!"

(A) *Howard the Duck*
(B) *Pretty in Pink*
(C) *Sixteen Candles*
(D) *Some Kind of Wonderful*
(E) *National Lampoon's Class Reunion*

148. Someone says, "Yo, Darnell — check out this Truckster. It's got a luggage rack."

(A) *The Great Outdoors*
(B) *Planes, Trains and Automobiles*
(C) *Uncle Buck*
(D) *National Lampoon's Vacation*
(E) *National Lampoon's Christmas Vacation*

149. Someone says, "Yo, Ahab."

(A) *Sixteen Candles*
(B) *Some Kind of Wonderful*
(C) *The Breakfast Club*
(D) *Ferris Bueller's Day Off*
(E) *National Lampoon's Class Reunion*

150. Introducing Macaulay Culkin!

(A) *Uncle Buck*
(B) *Planes, Trains and Automobiles*
(C) *The Great Outdoors*
(D) *Mr. Mom*
(E) *She's Having a Baby*

151. Someone says, "Those aren't pillows!"

(A) *Sixteen Candles*
(B) *Planes, Trains and Automobiles*
(C) *The Great Outdoors*
(D) *National Lampoon's European Vacation*
(E) *She's Having a Baby*

152. The main characters appear on a game show called *Pig in a Poke.*

(A) *National Lampoon's Class Reunion*
(B) *Planes, Trains and Automobiles*
(C) *Mr. Mom*
(D) *National Lampoon's European Vacation*
(E) *She's Having a Baby*

GO ON TO THE NEXT PAGE

153. Someone says, "Yes, you are a total fag."

(A) *Pretty in Pink*
(B) *Sixteen Candles*
(C) *Weird Science*
(D) *Some Kind of Wonderful*
(E) *Uncle Buck*

154. Someone says, "In the family jewels?"

(A) *The Breakfast Club*
(B) *National Lampoon's Christmas Vacation*
(C) *Pretty in Pink*
(D) *Sixteen Candles*
(E) *Weird Science*

155. Someone says, "It was this morning, moron. Of course I remember."

(A) *The Great Outdoors*
(B) *Planes, Trains and Automobiles*
(C) *She's Having a Baby*
(D) *Some Kind of Wonderful*
(E) *Uncle Buck*

Questions 156–165 below consist of a description of a scene in a Steven Spielberg film, followed by five lettered movies.

Choose the movie that best fits the description.

156. Audrey Hepburn shows up as an angel.

(A) *Empire of the Sun*
(B) *Twilight Zone — The Movie*
(C) *Poltergeist*
(D) *Always*
(E) *The Color Purple*

157. Random quote: "Only the penitent man shall pass."

(A) *Raiders of the Lost Ark*
(B) *Indiana Jones and the Last Crusade*
(C) *Always*
(D) *An American Tail*
(E) *Poltergeist*

158. A main character gets drunk on beer.

(A) *Poltergeist*
(B) *Gremlins*
(C) *Raiders of the Lost Ark*
(D) **batteries not included*
(E) *E.T.: The Extra-Terrestrial*

159. Something called a "mogwai" figures in the plot.

(A) *Empire of the Sun*
(B) *Gremlins*
(C) *The Color Purple*
(D) *Indiana Jones and the Temple of Doom*
(E) *An American Tail*

GO ON TO THE NEXT PAGE

160. Spielberg's ex-wife, Amy Irving, is involved.

(A) *Young Sherlock Holmes*
(B) *Poltergeist*
(C) *Indiana Jones and the Temple of Doom*
(D) *Who Framed Roger Rabbit*
(E) *Innerspace*

161. Features Dan Aykroyd in an airport scene.

(A) *Always*
(B) *Indiana Jones and the Last Crusade*
(C) *Raiders of the Lost Ark*
(D) *The Color Purple*
(E) *Twilight Zone — The Movie*

162. Corey Feldman is in it sans Corey Haim.

(A) *Empire of the Sun*
(B) *Poltergeist*
(C) **batteries not included*
(D) *Always*
(E) *The Goonies*

163. It received an Oscar nomination for best picture.

(A) *Who Framed Roger Rabbit*
(B) *Empire of the Sun*
(C) *Always*
(D) *Poltergeist*
(E) *Raiders of the Lost Ark*

164. Ben Stiller is in it.

(A) *Empire of the Sun*
(B) *The Goonies*
(C) **batteries not included*
(D) *E.T.: The Extra-Terrestrial*
(E) *Twilight Zone — The Movie*

165. Someone says, "Ha ha. Very funny. Very funny."

(A) *Indiana Jones and the Temple of Doom*
(B) *The Goonies*
(C) *Gremlins*
(D) *Innerspace*
(E) *E.T.: The Extra-Terrestrial*

Spielberg, Part II

And just because he's the Man, here are a few more questions about Steven Spielberg. Rank these films in order of gross receipts:

166. ———	(A)	*Raiders of the Lost Ark*
167. ———	(B)	*Gremlins*
168. ———	(C)	*Indiana Jones and the Temple of Doom*
169. ———	(D)	*Indiana Jones and the Last Crusade*
170. ———	(E)	*E.T.: The Extra-Terrestrial*

GO ON TO THE NEXT PAGE

Oscar picks

Directions: The following section tests your knowledge of 1980s Academy Awards. Each question below contains a category in bold, followed by five lettered movies or people. Choose the movie or person ▓ does not fit with the category.

171. Best Picture

(A) *Gandhi*
(B) *Chariots of Fire*
(C) *The Last Emperor*
(D) *A Passage to India*
(E) *Amadeus*

172. Best Picture

(A) *Rain Man*
(B) *Out of Africa*
(C) *A Room with a View*
(D) *Driving Miss Daisy*
(E) *Platoon*

173. Best Director

(A) Woody Allen
(B) Barry Levinson
(C) Oliver Stone
(D) Warren Beatty
(E) Robert Redford

174. Best Actor

(A) Henry Fonda
(B) Ben Kingsley
(C) Robert Duvall
(D) F. Murray Abraham
(E) Jack Nicholson

175. Best Actor

(A) John Hurt
(B) Robert De Niro
(C) Michael Douglas
(D) Paul Newman
(E) Dustin Hoffman

176. Best Actress

(A) Cher
(B) Sally Field
(C) Diane Keaton
(D) Meryl Streep
(E) Shirley MacLaine

177. Best Actress

(A) Jodie Foster
(B) Sissy Spacek
(C) Marlee Matlin
(D) Glenn Close
(E) Jessica Tandy

178. Best Supporting Actor

(A) Michael Caine
(B) Morgan Freeman
(C) Louis Gossett, Jr.
(D) Kevin Kline
(E) Denzel Washington

179. Best Supporting Actress

(A) Linda Hunt
(B) Geena Davis
(C) Mary Steenburgen
(D) Jessica Lange
(E) Meryl Streep

180. Best Song

(A) "Fame"
(B) "I Just Called to Say I Love You"
(C) "Against All Odds"
(D) "Arthur's Theme (Best That You Can Do)"
(E) "Flashdance . . . What a Feeling"

GO ON TO THE NEXT PAGE

Willi██ Sanderson,
the Bard of Newhart

He may not be a household name, but William Sanderson definitely had it going on in the '80s. His most memorable role was that of Larry, the talkative brother of mutes Darryl and Darryl on the long-lasting sitcom *Newhart*. But Sanderson, a cornpone thespian, also had great roles in these three important '80s films:

Coal Miner's Daughter (1980) — Sanderson began the decade playing rumrun-
ning moonshiner Lee Dollarhide in this movie about Loretta Lynn.
Screen time: minimal.
Fate: shot by mountain outlaws.

Blade Runner (1982)
Just prior to *Newhart,* Sanderson landed the role of J. F. Sebastian
in the futuristic Harrison Ford flick *Blade Runner.*
Screen time: minimal.
Fate: killed by Daryl Hannah's android assassin. (Did someone say Daryl?)

Fletch (1985)
Sanderson's greatest role, that of real-estate swindler Jim Swarthout,
came after his face had become well known on *Newhart.*
Memorable dialogue: "Oh, are you a friend of Alan's?"
Screen time: minimal.
Fate: burgled and taken advantage of by Igor Stravinsky (a.k.a. Fletch).

GO ON TO THE NEXT PAGE

Fill in the blanks

Directions: Each sentence below has one or two blanks, each blank indicating that something has been omitted. Beneath the sentence are five lettered items or sets of items. Choose the answer for each blank that best fits the meaning of the sentence as a whole.

Questions 181–190 refer to
movie musicians.

Just like Jack Wagner and Patrick Swayze attempting to sing, '80s musicians felt the need to try out their acting ability. Their success was usually hit-or-miss; for every "She's Like the Wind" there was a failing "Heartbeat."

181. If you don't know ██████ e starred in —————, close this ██████ t now.

  (A) *Disorderlies*
  (B) *Sid & Nancy*
  (C) *Purple Rain*
  (D) *The Last Dragon*
  (E) *Action Jackson*

182. ███ a lawyer in ————, Cher got Liam Neeson off.

  (A) *Moonstruck*
  (B) *The Witches of Eastwick*
  (C) *Silkwood*
  (D) *Mask*
  (E) *Suspect*

183. Saxophonist ————— tooted a different horn in Jim Jarmusch's *Down by Law* and *Stranger Than Paradise.*

  (A) Evan Lurie
  (B) John Lurie
  (C) David Sanborn
  (D) Kenny G
  (E) Clarence Clemons

184. ————— was just around the corner from the *Light of Day,* yeah.

  (A) Belinda Carlisle
  (B) Joan Jett
  (C) Susanna Hoffs
  (D) Janet Jackson
  (E) Moon Unit Zappa

GO ON TO THE NEXT PAGE ▷

185. Sheila E. drummed up a decent perfomance in —————.

(A) *Krush Groove*
(B) *Under the Cherry Moon*
(C) *Purple Rain*
(D) *Breakin' 2: Electric Boogaloo*
(E) *Breakin'*

186. Madonna said, "Creep of the eighties!" to a guy in —————.

(A) *Desperately Seeking Susan*
(B) *Vision Quest*
(C) *Shanghai Surprise*
(D) *Who's That Girl?*
(E) *Bloodhounds of Broadway*

187. ————— was goofy Cyndi Lauper's star vehicle; goofy ————— had *UHF.*

(A) *The Tall Guy;* Weird Al Yankovic
(B) *The Goonies;* Weird Al Yankovic
(C) *No Holds Barred;* Weird Al Yankovic
(D) *Vibes;* Weird Al Yankovic
(E) *Overboard;* Elvis Costello

188. Susanna Hoffs's brief, painful foray into film was in ————— ; *Nomads* began —————'s film career.

(A) *Light of Day;* Morrissey
(B) *Under the Cherry Moon;* Billy Idol
(C) *Hard to Hold;* Michael Hutchence
(D) *Satisfaction;* Gary Numan
(E) *The Allnighter;* Adam Ant

189. In ————— , English singer ————— went around yelling, "I will kill him! I will kill him!"

(A) *The Bride;* Sting
(B) *Labyrinth;* David Bowie
(C) *Dune;* Sting
(D) *Merry Christmas, Mr. Lawrence;* David Bowie
(E) *Scandal;* Roland Gift

190. Martin Scorsese's *The Last Temptation of Christ* featured ————— as Pontius Pilate; *Bill & Ted's Excellent Adventure* gave ————— her chance to be Joan of Arc.

(A) David Bowie; Sinéad O'Connor
(B) John Lydon; Nancy Spungen
(C) John Lurie; Susanna Hoffs
(D) David Bowie; Jane Wiedlin
(E) Iggy Pop; Kate Bush

GO ON TO THE NEXT PAGE

Questions 191–200 refer to
teenagers in lust.

Teenagers seemed to be at their horniest in the 1980s, at least on film. From *Porky's* to *Private School,* these teen sex comedies usually featured plenty of nudity and double entendres. So much, in fact, that many impressionable young males learned the birds and the bees not from their parents but from movies just like these.

191. ———— was, like, *totally bodacious* in *Valley Girl.*

   (A) Christopher Atkins
   (B) Nicolas Cage
   (C) Peter Billingsley
   (D) Sean Penn
   (E) Zach Galligan

192. Heather Thomas is the object of Scott Baio's lust in ———— .

   (A) *My Chauffeur*
   (B) *Private Lessons*
   (C) *Zapped!*
   (D) *Screwballs*
   (E) *My Tutor*

193. Talk about horny! Whenever ———— gets randy in *My Demon Lover,* he sprouts horns.

   (A) Tim Robbins
   (B) Jon Cryer
   (C) Scott Valentine
   (D) Jason Bateman
   (E) Robert Downey, Jr.

194. If you wanted to catch Dan Monahan in action, you might rent ———— .

   (A) *Senior Week*
   (B) *Porky's 2: The Next Day*
   (C) *Class*
   (D) *Hardbodies*
   (E) *Hunk*

195. Rob Morrow and ———— get hot and horny in *Private Resort,* though thankfully not with each other.

   (A) Maxwell Caulfield
   (B) Brad Pitt
   (C) Bronson Pinchot
   (D) Johnny Depp
   (E) Rob Lowe

196. Some of the lusty teenagers in ———— are a tad upset when they get "crabs."

   (A) *Hot Moves*
   (B) *Spring Break*
   (C) *The Wild Life*
   (D) *Porky's*
   (E) *The Last American Virgin*

197. In ———— , a Japanese guy says, "Your breasts are like Mt. Fuji."

   (A) *Hot Dog . . . The Movie!*
   (B) *Meatballs 2*
   (C) *Sixteen Candles*
   (D) *Where the Boys Are '84*
   (E) *Paradise*

GO ON TO THE NEXT PAGE

198. Probably the most popular of the horny teen movies was ———— , in which ———— slept with a guy named Damone.

(A) *Blue Lagoon;* Brooke Shields
(B) *Youngblood;* Cynthia Gibb
(C) *Weird Science;* Kelly LeBrock
(D) *Private School;* Phoebe Cates
(E) *Fast Times at Ridgemont High;* Jennifer Jason Leigh

199. In ———— , Kevin Bacon and the gang summer at Camp ———— .

(A) *Poison Ivy;* Cucamunga
(B) *Meatballs Part II;* Sasquatch
(C) *Foxes;* Ticonderoga
(D) *Little Darlings;* Ponderosa
(E) *Friday the 13th;* Crystal Lake

200. ———— hits Palm Springs in *Fraternity Vacation;* Tom Cruise's getaway ———— in *Losin' It.*

(A) Judge Reinhold; Fort Lauderdale
(B) Tim Robbins; Tijuana
(C) Kevin Costner; Miami
(D) Bobcat Goldthwait; San Padre Island
(E) Charlie Sheen; Tijuana

S OP!

You have reached the e of Section II

Tunes

'80S PCAT PENCIL

Music math

Directions: The following questions test your mathematical music knowledge. You don't need to know much about math to answer them, but it would help if you know the numerical quantities from '80s music. From the five lettered answers, select the one that solves the equation given in the question.

1. Multiply the number of members in the Thompson Twins by 6, divide by 2, and subtract 3. What do you get?

(A) 0
(B) 3
(C) 6
(D) 9
(E) 15

2. Add one to the number of Bananarama members and multiply the sum by the number of INXS members. What is the result?

(A) 15
(B) 16
(C) 18
(D) 24
(E) 28

3. Subtract the last David Lee Roth Van Halen album from the first Sammy Hagar Van Halen album and what do you get?

(A) 1
(B) 15
(C) 3066
(D) 3166
(E) 6136

4. If you add the digits of the phone number that Tommy Tutone sang about in its only hit, what do you get?

(A) 38
(B) 39
(C) 40
(D) 43
(E) 46

GO ON TO THE NEXT PAGE

5. Replace *x* with the number of *Luftballons* that Nena sang about in her only hit in the formula $y = 2/3x \div 2$. What is *y*?

(A) 11
(B) 22
(C) 25
(D) 33
(E) 44

6. If you multiply the number after the word "Timbuk" in the group that sang "The Future's So Bright, I Gotta Wear Shades" by the title of Paul Hardcastle's Vietnam-inspired hit, what do you get?

(A) 2
(B) 36
(C) 38
(D) 51
(E) 57

7. How many years separate both the titles of a certain Prince album and a certain Eurythmics album as well as that same Eurythmics album and a year in the title of a Bryan Adams song?

(A) 12
(B) 15
(C) 36
(D) 99
(E) 100

8. Haircut 100's only hit in the United States had an equation in its title. If you replace the word "love" in the equation with the number in the last name of Mötley Crüe's bassist, what do you get?

(A) 1
(B) 4
(C) 7
(D) 108
(E) 2,005

Name the musical guru

Directions: Questions 9–20 ask you to name the musical guru behind the scenes. You are to look at the song and artist and choose:

(A)   if Prince had anything to do with the song
(B)   if Rick James had anything to do with the song
(C)   if Michael Jackson had anything to do with the song
(D)   if none of the three had anything to do with the song

Note: Since there are only four choices, it would be pretty dumb to mark (E).

9. "We're Not Gonna Take It," Twisted Sister

10. "The Glamorous Life," Sheila E.

11. "We Are the World," USA for Africa

12. "Rhythm of the Night," DeBarge

13. "Jungle Love," The Time

14. "In My House," The Mary Jane Girls

15. "Manic Monday," The Bangles

GO ON TO THE NEXT PAGE

16. "I Feel for You," Chaka Khan

17. "Somebody's Watching Me," Rockwell

18. "Sugar Walls," Sheena Easton

19. "Party All the Time," Eddie Murphy

20. "We Don't Have to Take Our Clothes Off," Jermaine Stewart

The Parentheticals
(Already!)

There was an unwritten rule for '80s musicians that they had to put some part of a song title in parentheses. What other reason for "You Should Be Mine (The Woo Woo Song)" by Jeffrey Osborne? Couldn't Mr. Osborne have just called it "The Woo Woo Song"? And what about Aerosmith's "Dude (Looks Like a Lady)"? Why not just call it "Dude Looks Like a Lady"? And would it have hurt Was (Not Was) to lose the punctuation in its name? Here's a list of some of the more pathetic parentheticals:

All Night Long (All Night)
Lionel Richie

Back to Life (However Do You Want Me)
Soul II Soul

Brass in Pocket (I'm Special)
The Pretenders

The Breakup Song (They Don't Write 'Em)
Greg Kihn Band

Caribbean Queen (No More Love on the Run)
Billy Ocean

Catch Me (I'm Falling)
Pretty Poison

Don't Know What You Got (Till It's Gone)
Cinderella

Don't You (Forget About Me)
Simple Minds

 GO ON TO THE NEXT PAGE

 **GO ON TO THE NEXT PAGE**

... more of

(ENOUGH WITH . . . PARENTHETICA...)

Dude (Looks Like a Lady)
Aerosmith

Edge of Seventeen (Just Like the White Winged Dove)
Stevie Nicks

Empty Garden (Hey Hey Johnny)
Elton John

Falling in Love (Uh-Oh)
Miami Sound Machine

(Forever) Live and Die
Orchestral Manoeuvres in the Dark

A Girl in Trouble (Is a Temporary Thing)
Romeo Void

Here I Am (Just When I Thought I Was Over You)
Air Supply

(How to Be a) Millionaire
ABC

I Can't Go for That (No Can Do)
Daryl Hall and John Oates

(I Just) Died in Your Arms
Cutting Crew

I Keep Forgettin' (Every Time You're Near)
Michael McDonald

I Knew You Were Waiting (for Me)
Aretha Franklin and George Michael

I Ran (So Far Away)
A Flock of Seagulls

Lyric ID

Directions: You're in the shower, and suddenly you belt out a few lyrics. But you can't remember where you heard them. Or can you? Questions 21–62 ask you to read the lyric and choose the correct artist and song title from the five lettered possibilities. (Bonus fun: See if you can get the lyric before looking at the five choices.)

21. "hit me with those laser beams"

    (A) "Rockit," Herbie Hancock
    (B) "Relax," Frankie Goes to Hollywood
    (C) "Bizarre Love Triangle," New Order
    (D) "Electric Avenue," Eddy Grant
    (E) "Mr. Roboto," Styx

22. "as sure as Kilimanjaro rises like Olympus above the Serengeti"

    (A) "Running Up That Hill," Kate Bush
    (B) "Jungle Love," The Time
    (C) "Don't Cry," Asia
    (D) "Walk Like an Egyptian," The Bangles
    (E) "Africa," Toto

23. "I think they got your alias"

    (A) "Owner of a Lonely Heart," Yes
    (B) "One Step Beyond," Madness
    (C) "Gloria," Laura Branigan
    (D) "Let's Go All the Way," Sly Fox
    (E) "Sunday Bloody Sunday," U2

24. "buying bread from a man in Brussels"

    (A) "Key Largo," Bertie Higgins
    (B) "All You Can Eat," The Fat Boys
    (C) "Down Under," Men at Work
    (D) "I Eat Cannibals (Part 1)," Total Coelo
    (E) "I Beg Your Pardon," Kon Kan

GO ON TO THE NEXT PAGE

GO ON TO THE NEXT PAGE

25. "I knew he must have been about seventeen"

   (A) "I Love Rock 'n Roll," Joan Jett and the Blackhearts
   (B) "All Those Years Ago," George Harrison
   (C) "Making Plans for Nigel," XTC
   (D) "(She's) Sexy +17," The Stray Cats
   (E) "Buffalo Stance," Neneh Cherry

26. "everyone's a superhero, everyone's a Captain Kirk"

   (A) "Der Kommissar," Falco
   (B) "Rock You Like a Hurricane," Scorpions
   (C) "Major Tom (Coming Home)," Peter Schilling
   (D) "Vienna Calling," Falco
   (E) "99 Luftballons," Nena

27. "You don't drink, don't smoke, what do you do?"

   (A) "Goody Two Shoes," Adam Ant
   (B) "We Don't Have to Take Our Clothes Off," Jermaine Stewart
   (C) "Super Freak (Part 1)," Rick James
   (D) "Like a Virgin," Madonna
   (E) "Shake It Up," The Cars

28. "there's nothing left to talk about unless it's horizontally"

   (A) "I Need Love," L. L. Cool J
   (B) "Let's Go to Bed," The Cure
   (C) "Sex (I'm a . . .)," Berlin
   (D) "Sexual Healing," Marvin Gaye
   (E) "Physical," Olivia Newton-John

29. "but the man from Mars is through with cars"

   (A) "Pump Up the Volume," M/A/R/R/S
   (B) "Illegal Alien," Genesis
   (C) "Ashes to Ashes," David Bowie
   (D) "Rapture," Blondie
   (E) "Cars," Gary Neuman

. . . more of

(ENOUGH WITH) THE PARENTHETICALS (ALREADY!)

I Wanna Dance with Somebody (Who Loves Me)
Whitney Houston

It's Not Over ('Til It's Over)
Starship

(I've Had) The Time of My Life
Bill Medley and Jennifer Warnes

Jump (for My Love)
The Pointer Sisters

(Just Like) Starting Over
John Lennon

(Keep Feeling) Fascination
The Human League

Lady (You Bring Me Up)
The Commodores

Major Tom (Coming Home)
Peter Schilling

Master Blaster (Jammin')
Stevie Wonder

Morning Train (Nine to Five)
Sheena Easton

Naughty Girls (Need Love Too)
Samantha Fox

Opportunities (Let's Make Lots of Money)
Pet Shop Boys

Pride (In the Name of Love)
U2

GO ON TO THE NEXT PAGE

GO ON TO THE NEXT PAGE

...more of
(ENOUGH WITH) THE PARENTHETICALS (ALREADY!)

Rock Me Tonight (for Old Times Sake)
Freddie Jackson

Separate Ways (Worlds Apart)
Journey

She's a Bad Mama Jama (She's Built, She's Stacked)
Carl Carlton

(She's) Sexy + 17
The Stray Cats

Silent Running (On Dangerous Ground)
Mike + the Mechanics

Sweet Dreams (Are Made of This)
Eurythmics

The Sweetest Thing (I've Ever Known)
Juice Newton

There'll Be Sad Songs (to Make You Cry)
Billy Ocean

Time (Clock of the Heart)
Culture Club

Tonight I'm Yours (Don't Hurt Me)
Rod Stewart

Touch Me (I Want Your Body)
Samantha Fox

Train in Vain (Stand by Me)
The Clash

What's on Your Mind (Pure Energy)
Information Society

30. "just try to understand, I've given all I can"

   (A) "A Little Respect," Erasure
   (B) "Borderline," Madonna
   (C) "Bette Davis Eyes," Kim Carnes
   (D) "Don't Let's Start," They Might Be Giants
   (E) "She-Bop," Cyndi Lauper

31. "domo origato"

   (A) "China Girl," David Bowie
   (B) "Mr. Roboto," Styx
   (C) "Turning Japanese," The Vapors
   (D) "Why Me?," Planet P
   (E) "Sweet Dreams (Are Made of This)," Eurythmics

32. "Just a city boy, born and raised in South Detroit"

   (A) "Morning Train (Nine to Five)," Sheena Easton
   (B) "Don't Stop Believin'," Journey
   (C) "The Metro," Berlin
   (D) "Hold On to the Nights," Richard Marx
   (E) "Shattered Dreams," Johnny Hates Jazz

33. " 'cause I got such a long way to go to make it to the border of Mexico"

   (A) "Don't Forget Me (When I'm Gone)," Glass Tiger
   (B) "La Bamba," Los Lobos
   (C) "Mexican Radio," Wall of Voodoo
   (D) "Come Go with Me," Exposé
   (E) "Ride Like the Wind," Christopher Cross

GO ON TO THE NEXT PAGE

GO ON TO THE NEXT PAGE

34. "Damned if I do, damned if I don't"

(A) "Workin' for a Livin'," Huey Lewis and the News
(B) "Edge of Seventeen (Just Like the White Winged Dove)," Stevie Nicks
(C) "Leave It," Yes
(D) "What Have You Done for Me Lately?" Janet Jackson
(E) "Dirty Laundry," Don Henley

35. "my country 'tis of thee, sweet land of liberty"

(A) "Hooked on Classics," The Royal Philharmonic Orchestra
(B) "In a Big Country," Big Country
(C) "America," Neil Diamond
(D) "Vacation," The Go-Go's
(E) "Kids in America," Kim Wilde

36. "it's a big enough umbrella"

(A) "Here Comes the Rain Again," Eurythmics
(B) "Life in a Northern Town," The Dream Academy
(C) "Blame It on the Rain," Milli Vanilli
(D) "She's Like the Wind," Patrick Swayze (featuring Wendy Fraser)
(E) "Evey Little Thing She Does Is Magic," The Police

. . . more of

(ENOUGH WITH) THE PARENTHETICALS (ALREADY!)

Whisper to a Scream (Birds Fly)
Icicle Works

Wishing (I Had a Photograph of You)
A Flock of Seagulls

**You Can't Get What You Want
(Till You Know What You Want)**
Joe Jackson

You Got It (The Right Stuff)
New Kids on the Block

You're Only Human (Second Wind)
Billy Joel

You Should Be Mine (The Woo Woo Song)
Jeffrey Osborne

AND

THE PARENTHETICAL POOBAH AWARD

goes to:

(You Gotta) Fight for Your Right (to Party!)

The Beastie Boys

GO ON TO THE NEXT PAGE

37. "Where can I find a woman like that!?"

  (A) "Joanna," Kool & the Gang
  (B) "She's On It," The Beastie Boys
  (C) "Jessie's Girl," Rick Springfield
  (D) "The Lady in Red," Chris De Burgh
  (E) "Sophisticated Bitch," Public Enemy

38. "Out on the road today, I saw a Deadhead sticker on a Cadillac"

  (A) "Freeway of Love," Aretha Franklin
  (B) "Faithfully," Journey
  (C) "The Boys of Summer," Don Henley
  (D) "Kiss Me Deadly," Lita Ford
  (E) "Touch of Grey," The Grateful Dead

39. "giddy-up-a-oom-papa-oom-papa-mow-mow"

  (A) "Elvira," The Oak Ridge Boys
  (B) "Ricky," Weird Al Yankovic
  (C) "The Devil Went Down to Georgia," The Charlie Daniels Band
  (D) "Wake Me Up Before You Go-Go," Wham!
  (E) "Shaddup You Face," Joe Dolce Music Theatre

40. "I had a dream, I had an awesome dream"

  (A) "Say You Will," Foreigner
  (B) "Voices," Russ Ballard
  (C) "The Best of Times," Styx
  (D) "Almost Paradise . . . Theme from *Footloose*," Mike Reno and Ann Wilson
  (E) "Say You, Say Me," Lionel Richie

41. "the dream we all dream of: Boy vs. Girl in the World Series of Love"

  (A) "Funky Town," Pseudo Echo
  (B) "Centerfield," John Fogerty
  (C) "I'm Goin' Down," Bruce Springsteen
  (D) "All Night Long (All Night)," Lionel Richie
  (E) "U Got the Look," Prince

42. "When I'm walking, I strut my stuff and I'm so strung out"

  (A) "Glamour Boys," Living Colour
  (B) "Blister in the Sun," Violent Femmes
  (C) "God Is a Bullet," Concrete Blonde
  (D) "Senses Working Overtime," XTC
  (E) "One Thing Leads to Another," The Fixx

43. "at night I wake up with the sheets soaking wet"

  (A) "I'm on Fire," Bruce Springsteen
  (B) "One Night in Bangkok," Murray Head
  (C) "Infatuation," Rod Stewart
  (D) "Obsession," Animotion
  (E) "Voices Carry," 'Til Tuesday

44. "you play with words, you play with love"

  (A) "Fortress Around Your Heart," Sting
  (B) "How Will I Know," Whitney Houston
  (C) "Kiss," Prince and the Revolution
  (D) "Private Eyes," Hall and Oates
  (E) "Gloria," Laura Branigan

45. "Welcome to your life. There's no turning back."

  (A) "Midnight Blue," Lou Gramm
  (B) "Shiny Shiny," Haysi Fantayzee
  (C) "Everybody Wants to Rule the World," Tears for Fears
  (D) "Train in Vain (Stand by Me)," The Clash
  (E) "AEIOU Sometimes Y," EBN-OZN

46. "you see it all around you — good lovin' gone bad"

  (A) "I'll Wait," Van Halen
  (B) "When It's Love," Van Halen
  (C) "Is This Love," Whitesnake
  (D) "Hold On Loosely," .38 Special
  (E) "Under Pressure," Queen and David Bowie

GO ON TO THE NEXT PAGE

47. "hanging out by the state line turning holy water into wine"

(A) "I Can't Drive 55," Sammy Hagar
(B) "Eyes Without a Face," Billy Idol
(C) "Me and My Wine," Def Leppard
(D) "Fantasy," Aldo Nova
(E) "You've Got Another Thing Comin'," Judas Priest

48. "I am the son and the heir of a shyness that is criminally vulgar"

(A) "Robert De Niro's Waiting," Bananarama
(B) "Jane Says," Jane's Addiction
(C) "Closer to Fine," Indigo Girls
(D) "How Soon Is Now?" The Smiths
(E) "Forever Young," Alphaville

49. "those five years we have had have been such good times"

(A) "Never Surrender," Corey Hart
(B) "Eternal Flame," the Bangles
(C) "Don't You Want Me," The Human League
(D) "Girl You Know It's True," Milli Vanilli
(E) "All Those Years Ago," George Harrison

50. "tin roof rusted"

(A) "Burning Down the House," Talking Heads
(B) "I Want Candy," Bow Wow Wow
(C) "In My House," The Mary Jane Girls
(D) "Love Shack," The B-52's
(E) "House of Fun," Madness

51. "I get my kicks above the waistline, Sunshine"

(A) "That's What Friends Are For." Dionne & Friends
(B) "Keep Your Hands to Yourself," Georgia Satellites
(C) "One Night in Bangkok," Murray Head
(D) "I Ran (So Far Away)," A Flock of Seagulls
(E) "This Is Not a Love Song," PiL

52. "a lifetime spent preparing for the journey"

(A) "Sussudio," Phil Collins
(B) "Don't Pay the Ferryman," Chris De Burgh
(C) "The Chauffeur," Duran Duran
(D) "Brass in Pocket (I'm Special)," The Pretenders
(E) "She's a Beauty," The Tubes

53. "Marconi plays the mamba"

(A) "Conga," Miami Sound Machine
(B) "When Smokey Sings," ABC
(C) "We Built This City," Starship
(D) "Radio Ga-Ga," Queen
(E) "You Spin Me Round (Like a Record)," Dead or Alive

54. "I walked along the avenue; I never thought I'd meet a girl like you"

(A) "Just Got Lucky," JoBoxers
(B) "Master and Servant," Depeche Mode
(C) "I Ran (So Far Away)," A Flock of Seagulls
(D) "Baby Don't Forget My Number," Milli Vanilli
(E) "Some Like It Hot," Power Station

55. "When I saw her smile across a crowded room, I knew we'd have to leave the party soon"

(A) "Freeze-Frame," J. Geils Band
(B) "Going Back to Cali," L. L. Cool J
(C) "Out of Touch," Hall and Oates
(D) "The Boys of Summer," Don Henley
(E) "And We Danced," The Hooters

GO ON TO THE NEXT PAGE

56. "out of my window I could see them, two silhouettes saying goodnight"

(A) "Smalltown Boy," Bronski Beat
(B) "The Lady in Red," Chris De Burgh
(C) "Who's That Girl?" Eurythmics
(D) "Come Dancing," The Kinks
(E) "Don't Stand So Close to Me," The Police

57. "there's a stain on my notebook"

(A) "(I Just) Died in Your Arms," Cutting Crew
(B) "She Works Hard for the Money," Donna Summer
(C) "Manic Monday," The Bangles
(D) "Black Coffee in Bed," Squeeze
(E) "Something About You," Level 42

58. "keep me burnin' for your love, with the touch of a velvet glove"

(A) "Romanticide," Combo Audio
(B) "Abracadabra," The Steve Miller Band
(C) "Love Removal Machine," The Cult
(D) "Never Say Never," Romeo Void
(E) "Mountain Song," Jane's Addiction

59. "you're about as easy as a nuclear war"

(A) "Lips Like Sugar," Echo and the Bunnymen
(B) "Easy Lover," Philip Bailey with Phil Collins
(C) "Is There Something I Should Know," Duran Duran
(D) "When I See You Smile," Bad English
(E) "Let's Go All the Way," Sly Fox

60. "got killed by ten million pounds of sludge from New York and New Jersey"

(A) "And the Walls Came Down," The Call
(B) "Brand New Lover," Dead or Alive
(C) "New World Man," Rush
(D) "Monkey Gone to Heaven," The Pixies
(E) "Radioactive," The Firm

61. "take a look at my face, and see what you're doing to me"

(A) "Foolish Beat," Debbie Gibson
(B) "Loverboy," Billy Ocean
(C) "All Cried Out," Lisa Lisa and Cult Jam with Full Force
(D) "Walking on a Thin Line," Huey Lewis and the News
(E) "Against All Odds (Take a Look at Me Now)," Phil Collins

62. "My first impulse was to run up on ya and do a Rambo"

(A) "Eye of the Tiger," Survivor
(B) "Far From Over," Frank Stallone
(C) "No Sleep Till Brooklyn," The Beastie Boys
(D) "The Rain," Oran "Juice" Jones
(E) "Go See the Doctor," Kool Moe Dee

GO ON TO THE NEXT PAGE

Jon Bon Jovi vs. Bruce Springsteen
Who Won?

They're both pretty Jersey boys with distinguished music careers,
but in a tale of ten categories, who's "goin' down"?

Category	Jon Bon Jovi	Bruce Springsteen	Winner
Origin	Sayreville, New Jersey	Freehold, New Jersey	pick 'em
Signature	"You Give Love a Bad Name"	"Born in the U.S.A."	Bruce
Number 1s	four	zero (!)	Bon Jovi
Biggest hit	"Livin' on a Prayer"	"Dancing in the Dark"	Bon Jovi
Other hit	"Wanted Dead or Alive"	"I'm on Fire"	Bruce
Dumb album title	*Slippery When Wet*	*Tunnel of Love*	Bon Jovi
Nickname	none	"The Boss"	Bruce
Band member	Richie Sambora	Clarence Clemons	Bruce
Look	ripped jeans, toussled hair	tight jeans, unkempt hair	pick 'em
Marriage	high-school sweetheart	Julianne Phillips	Bon Jovi
Tiebreaker:			
Confused with	lead singer of White Lion	Rick Springfield	Bruce

"The Boss"
wins!

GO ON TO THE NEXT PAGE

Duran Duran story problem

Directions: After reading the passage about Duran Duran below, answer the six questions that follow it.

The Fab Five are putting on makeup before the
video shoot for their next single. Nick Rhodes, the
keyboardist, turns to the lead singer and asks,
"Do you have any more mascara? Mine's bone-dry."
[5]   *The singer says, "Borrow one of the Taylors'.*
Mine doesn't go with your eyeliner."
  Nick turns to Roger Taylor. "Give us some of yours,
will you, Rog?"
  Roger says, "Get your own, you fruit. My therapist
[10] *says we all have to forge our own identity."*
  John interrupts. "Here, Nick. You can borrow
mine. Roger's just scared you'll look better than he
will. He's not getting millions of fan letters like you
are, you know."
[15]   *"Shove your bass up your bum!" shouts Roger*
at John.
  The third Taylor says, "Cut it out, chaps. Listen:
don't you think this video's a bit silly? We don't take
off any clothes, we don't wrestle any women in the
[20] *jungle, we aren't sailing a yacht. We're just standing*
on stage waiting for a computer-generated wave to
flood the audience. It's rather dull, don't you think?"
  "Yeah," says the singer, "but think of the symbol-
ism. That wave is like our music. The fans are hot
[25] *and sweaty. They want that water on them. It's*
refreshing. We don't need to take our clothes off all
the time. Our fans are smart."
  John stifles a laugh. "What is he on about?"
  Nick says, "Who cares? Give me some lipstick!"

63. The author focuses primarily on ——— .

  (A) the role makeup plays in shooting music
       videos
  (B) the in-fighting of a major band of the
       '80s
  (C) why Duran Duran was a great band
  (D) symbolism in music videos
  (E) making Duran Duran sound as ridiculous
       as possible

64. In lines 5–6, the singer is ——— .

  (A) having a hissy fit
  (B) pointing out a possible fashion faux pas
       on the part of Nick Rhodes
  (C) named Simon LaBone
  (D) being a big fat liar
  (E) reveling in self-love

65. The third Taylor in line 17 is ——— .

  (A) Andy, the bassist
  (B) Patrick, the drummer
  (C) Alan, the guitarist
  (D) Andy, the guitarist
  (E) the band member with the biggest
       solo hit

66. The video described in line 18–22 is ——— .

  (A) "Notorious"
  (B) "New Moon on Monday"
  (C) "The Reflex"
  (D) "Wild Boys"
  (E) "Save a Prayer"

67. What band will Roger, Nick, and the singer
form less than two years after the video is
released?

  (A) Arcadia
  (B) Glass Tiger
  (C) The Power Station
  (D) Animal Logic
  (E) Tony! Toni! Tone!

GO ON TO THE NEXT PAGE

68. Which of the following can be inferred from the passage?

   I.   There are three people in the band with the last name Taylor.

   II. The band members all receive a lot of fan mail.

   III. The keyboardist wears a lot of makeup for a guy.

(A) I only
(B) II only
(C) III only
(D) I and II only
(E) I and III only

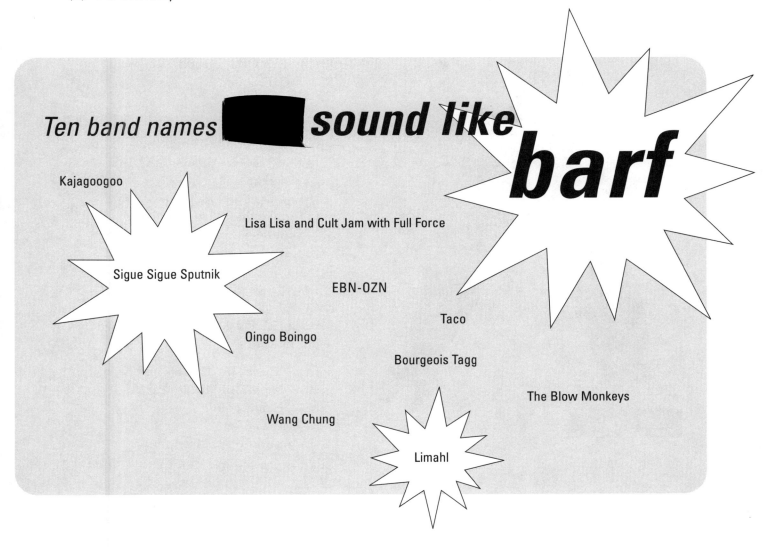

GO ON TO THE NEXT PAGE

Hall and Oates logic

Directions: After reading the passage about Hall and Oates below, answer the four questions that follow it.

Daryl Hall is taller, more talented, and better dressed than his partner, John Oates. He also has a golden voice. Simply stated, Hall would still be Hall without Oates, but Oates would be nothing without Hall. Starting with "Kiss on My List" and "You Make My Dreams," Hall literally carried his miniscule, mustachioed partner on a dizzying ride up the Billboard charts. And what about "Maneater," the catchiest song of all time? Yes, if he had been smarter, Hall would have gone solo long ago.

Hall & Oates

69. It can be inferred from the passage that ——— .

   (A) the author thinks Hall is stupid
   (B) the author thinks Oates is stupid
   (C) the author likes Oates better than Hall
   (D) Oates doesn't dress well
   (E) Oates probably wouldn't like it if he read it

70. Which of the following would most cripple the author's main argument?

   (A) A study of John Oates's solo history.
   (B) A study of Daryl Hall's solo history.
   (C) A rumor that the two were deeply in love.
   (D) That Hall couldn't have written "I Can't Go For That (No Can Do)" without Oates's input.
   (E) That Oates is good friends with G. E. Smith.

71. In ██████ argument, the author does all ██████ ng EXCEPT ——— .

   (A) present biased (and, let's face it, downright mean) information
   (B) praise Daryl Hall's musical talents
   (C) claim that "Maneater" is the best song of all time
   (D) say that Oates has facial hair
   (E) call John Oates short

72. Completely destroying the author's argument, when Hall did go solo in 1986, he had only one hit with ——— .

   (A) "You've Lost That Loving Feeling"
   (B) "Method of Modern Love"
   (C) "Family Man"
   (D) "Dreamtime"
   (E) "Since You're Gone"

GO ON TO THE NEXT PAGE

Whose lead singer are you?

Below are three groups of five questions. Each question consists of a singer (in Column A) and a band (in Column B). In each group, you are to match a singer in Column A to the band in Column B that he or she belongs to. (Note: Each band in Column B will be chosen only once per category.)

Questions 73–77 refer to cheese rock.

You are asked to match the mall rocker in Column A with the appropriate cheese band in Column B.

A	B
73. Mike Reno	(A) REO Speedwagon
74. Kim Wilson	(B) Cheap Trick
75. Robin Zander	(C) Loverboy
76. Ann Wilson	(D) Heart
77. Kevin Cronin	(E) The Fabulous Thunderbirds

Questions 78–82 refer to hard rock.

You are asked to match the screeching longhair in Column A with the appropriate hard-rockin' band in Column B.

A	B
78. Vince Neil	(A) Poison
79. Bret Michaels	(B) Mötley Crüe
80. David Coverdale	(C) Cinderella
81. Stephen Pearcy	(D) Whitesnake
82. Tom Keifer	(E) Ratt

Questions 83–87 refer to modern rock.

You are asked to match the mopey lead singer in Column A with the appropriate alternative band in Column B.

A	B
83. Morrissey	(A) The Cure
84. Bernard Sumner	(B) Echo and the Bunnymen
85. Ian McCulloch	(C) Bauhaus
86. Peter Murphy	(D) The Smiths
87. Robert Smith	(E) New Order

GO ON TO THE NEXT PAGE

Michael Jackson vs. Prince
Who Won?

Both singers used names that signified their music royalty, but they may as well have been from warring nations.
The Prince camp intensely disliked the King of Pop, and MJ wanted to cast Prince in the antagonistic
Wesley Snipes role in his "Bad" video (which would then have had Michael saying to Prince, "Your butt is mine").
If the two were to duke it out in the following ten categories,
the diminutive Prince would hold his own against the Pepsi-drinkin', llama-lovin' Jackson.
Still, though the outcome may be contested until the end of time, the billions of fans who cry
at MJ's concerts can't be wrong.

Category	*Michael Jackson*	*Prince*	*Winner*
Album	*Thriller*	*Purple Rain*	Michael Jackson
Biggest hit	"Billie Jean"	"When Doves Cry"	Michael Jackson
Other hit	"Beat It"	"Let's Go Crazy"	Prince
Ballad	"Human Nature"	"Purple Rain"	Prince
Duet with	Paul McCartney	Sheena Easton	Prince
Clothing	*Thriller* jacket	purple trenchcoat	Michael Jackson
Dancing	the Moonwalk	jump down, turn around	Michael Jackson
Best Video	*Thriller*	*Alphabet St.*	Michael Jackson
Disciple	Corey Feldman	Vanity	Prince
Likes	little boys	hot women	Prince
Tiebreaker:	"Mama say mama sah mamakusah"	"Dr. Everything'll be all right"	Michael Jackson

Michael Jackson
wins!

GO ON TO THE NEXT PAGE

The video game

Directions: Each passage below describes a scene in a music video from the '80s. From the five lettered choices that follow each passage, select the artist and song that best fits the description.

88. A man in a red jacket and his date take in a movie about a werewolf.

(A) "Ebony and Ivory," Paul McCartney and Stevie Wonder
(B) "Thriller," Michael Jackson
(C) "Through Being Cool," Devo
(D) "Voices Carry," 'Til Tuesday
(E) "Nasty," Janet Jackson

89. A bunch of cheerleaders are jumping around singing about some guy.

(A) "Jeanny," Falco
(B) "Mickey," Toni Basil
(C) "Be Good Johnny," Men at Work
(D) "Smooth Operator," Sade
(E) "Dude (Looks Like a Lady)," Aerosmith

90. A young woman gets sucked into a comic book and falls in love with its hero.

(A) "Fish Heads," Barnes & Barnes
(B) "Who's That Girl?" Eurythmics
(C) "Forever Your Girl," Paula Abdul
(D) "Take on Me," a-ha
(E) "(She's) Sexy + 17," The Stray Cats

91. Chevy Chase mugs for the camera.

(A) "I.G.Y. (What a Beautiful World)," Donald Fagen
(B) "You Can Call Me Al," Paul Simon
(C) "You Might Think," The Cars
(D) "Don't Worry Be Happy," Bobby McFerrin
(E) "Come Dancing," The Kinks

92. Some weirdos dance around a maypole.

(A) "You Got Lucky," Tom Petty and the Heartbreakers
(B) "The Safety Dance," Men Without Hats
(C) "True Faith," New Order
(D) "Girls Just Want to Have Fun," Cyndi Lauper
(E) "Dance Hall Days," Wang Chung

93. A young boy gets the carnival ride of his life.

(A) "Girls on Film," Duran Duran
(B) "She's a Beauty," The Tubes
(C) "Bust a Move," Young MC
(D) "Open Your Heart," Madonna
(E) "Shake It Up," The Cars

94. A white singer tussles with a scantily clad black woman in a jungle.

(A) "Love Plus One," Haircut 100
(B) "Tarzan Boy," Baltimora
(C) "Welcome to the Jungle," Guns N' Roses
(D) "Hungry Like the Wolf," Duran Duran
(E) "Shock the Monkey," Peter Gabriel

95. There's lots of mirrors and makeup and one of the most memorable haircuts ever captured on tape.

(A) "Love Missile F1–11," Sigue Sigue Sputnik
(B) "I Ran (So Far Away)," A Flock of Seagulls
(C) "I Want Candy," Bow Wow Wow
(D) "Words," Missing Persons
(E) "Love Song," The Cure

96. A bunch of prostitutes do a dance of defiance in front of their brothel owner.

(A) "Young Turks," Rod Stewart
(B) "Beat It," Michael Jackson
(C) "Love Is a Battlefield," Pat Benatar
(D) "Legs," ZZ Top
(E) "She Works Hard for the Money," Donna Summer

GO ON TO THE NEXT PAGE

97. A blind student sculpts a bust of a horny older man.

(A) "Hello," Lionel Richie
(B) "Don't Stand So Close to Me," The Police
(C) "Hot for Teacher," Van Halen
(D) "Centerfold," J. Geils Band
(E) "Somebody's Watching Me," Rockwell

98. Sex on the beach.

(A) "Mad About You," Belinda Carlisle
(B) "China Girl," David Bowie
(C) "I Want Your Sex," George Michael
(D) "Burning Up," Madonna
(E) "Rio," Duran Duran

99. Danny Aiello plays someone's father.

(A) "Papa Don't Preach," Madonna
(B) "Eye of the Tiger," Survivor
(C) "Valley Girl," Frank Zappa
(D) "If This Is It," Huey Lewis and the News
(E) "Twilight Zone," Golden Earring

100. Milton Berle appears, in drag.

(A) "Sister Christian," Night Ranger
(B) "Turn Me Loose," Loverboy
(C) "On the Loose," Saga
(D) "Smokin' in the Boys Room," Mötley Crüe
(E) "Round and Round," Ratt

101. The guy who played Niedermeier in *National Lampoon's Animal House* asks a high-school student, "What do you wanna do with your life?"

(A) "I Wanna Rock," Twisted Sister
(B) "Spies Like Us," Paul McCartney
(C) "We're Not Gonna Take It," Twisted Sister
(D) "Rock 'n' Roll High School," The Ramones
(E) "Eat It," Weird Al Yankovic

102. Someone hammers nails into a coffin in time to drumbeats.

(A) "Dancing with Myself," Billy Idol
(B) "Eyes Without a Face," Billy Idol
(C) "Rebel Yell," Billy Idol
(D) "White Wedding," Billy Idol
(E) All of the above

103. A woman dives into a pool with no water and emerges unscathed and wet.

(A) "Do You Really Want to Hurt Me," Culture Club
(B) "Caribbean Queen (No More Love on the Run)," Billy Ocean
(C) "Cuts Like a Knife," Bryan Adams
(D) "Infatuation," Rod Stewart
(E) "Magic," The Cars

104. Someone says, "He says, 'Kill me.' Over and over again — 'kill me.'"

(A) "Thriller," Michael Jackson
(B) "Welcome to the Jungle," Guns N' Roses
(C) "One," Metallica
(D) "Don't You Want Me," The Human League
(E) "Bark at the Moon," Ozzy Osbourne

105. Video featuring Waldo, a nerd.

(A) "Sussudio," Phil Collins
(B) "Hot for Teacher," Van Halen
(C) "Free Fallin'," Tom Petty and the Heartbreakers
(D) "Another Brick in the Wall (Part II)," Pink Floyd
(E) "(You Gotta) Fight for Your Right (to Party!)," The Beastie Boys

GO ON TO THE NEXT PAGE

106. There's a cow.

(A) "Sweet Dreams (Are Made of This),"
    Eurythmics
(B) "In a Big Country," Big Country
(C) "Rapture," Blondie
(D) "Nasty," Janet Jackson
(E) "Straight Up," Paula Abdul

107. There's an armadillo.

(A) "Gimme All Your Lovin'," ZZ Top
(B) "Electric Avenue," Eddy Grant
(C) "Hurts So Good," John Cougar
(D) "Rock the Casbah," The Clash
(E) "Mexican Radio," Wall of Voodoo

108. There's Courteney Cox.

(A) "Glory Days," Bruce Springsteen
(B) "Bop 'Til You Drop," Rick Springfield
(C) "Dancing in the Dark," Bruce
    Springsteen
(D) "Batdance," Prince
(E) "Dancing with Myself," Billy Idol

109. Rae Dawn Chong rides shotgun in a pickup
    truck driven by a British singer.

(A) "Blue Jean," David Bowie
(B) "Just Another Night," Mick Jagger
(C) "Too Late for Goodbyes," Julian Lennon
(D) "After the Fire," Roger Daltrey
(E) "Undercover of the Night," The Rolling
    Stones

We're #1,
We're #1

The following 241 songs (arranged in chronological order) all made it to the top spot on America's Top 40 Countdown. You know that Casey Kasem probably had a particularly inspiring story to relate about each one. Looking over the list, it's hard not to feel a little nostalgic, especially when you see the words "Rock Me Amadeus" (Falco, 1986).

1980

"Please Don't Go"
KC and the Sunshine Band

"Rock With You"
Michael Jackson

"Do That to Me One More Time"
The Captain & Tennille

"Crazy Little Thing Called Love"
Queen

"Another Brick in the Wall (Part II)"
Pink Floyd

"Call Me"
Blondie

"Funkytown"
Lipps, Inc.

"Coming Up (Live at Glasgow)"
Paul McCartney and Wings

GO ON TO THE NEXT PAGE

GO ON TO THE NEXT PAGE

...more of

"It's Still Rock and Roll to Me"
Billy Joel

"Magic"
Olivia Newton-John

"Sailing"
Christopher Cross

"Upside Down"
Diana Ross

"Another One Bites the Dust"
Queen

"Woman in Love"
Barbra Streisand

"Lady"
Kenny Rogers

"(Just Like) Starting Over"
John Lennon

1981

"The Tide Is High"
Blondie

"Celebration"
Kool & the Gang

"9 to 5"
Dolly Parton

"I Love a Rainy Night"
Eddie Rabbitt

110. A singer dressed up like a tribal warrior asks a convenience store clerk for "a glazed donut and a bottle of anything — to go."

   (A) "Welcome to the Jungle," Guns N' Roses
   (B) "Walk the Dinosaur," Was (Not Was)
   (C) "Eat It," Weird Al Yankovic
   (D) "Panama," Van Halen
   (E) "Yankee Rose," David Lee Roth

111. Michael J. Fox and Jami Gertz battle it out in a domestic squabble.

   (A) "Tarzan Boy," Baltimora
   (B) "The Power of Love," Huey Lewis and the News
   (C) "Light of Day," The Barbusters
   (D) "At This Moment," Billy Vera & the Beaters
   (E) "Stick Around," Julian Lennon

112. When a disgruntled singer walks out on an offer, a record producer asks, "Where are you going, Steve? The label loves it, Steve. Steve?!"

   (A) "Abracadabra," The Steve Miller Band
   (B) "Raised on Radio," Journey
   (C) "That Girl," Stevie Wonder
   (D) "Oh Sherrie," Steve Perry
   (E) "Angel," Aerosmith

GO ON TO THE NEXT PAGE

GO ON TO THE NEXT PAGE

Which doesn't fit?

Each question below consists of something in bold, followed by five lettered musicians or songs. Choose the lettered musician or song that does not fit with the bolded item.

Questions 113–122 refer to big causes.

113. Band Aid

(A) Simon Le Bon
(B) Phil Collins
(C) Kool & the Gang
(D) Pete Townshend
(E) Boy George

114. "That's What Friends Are For"

(A) Aretha Franklin
(B) Gladys Knight
(C) Stevie Wonder
(D) Elton John
(E) Dionne Warwick

115. Rockers at Live Aid (July 13, 1985)

(A) Journey
(B) REO Speedwagon
(C) George Thorogood and the Destroyers
(D) Ozzy Osbourne
(E) Judas Priest

116. British pop bands at Live Aid

(A) Simple Minds
(B) Tears for Fears
(C) The Thompson Twins
(D) Wham!
(E) Duran Duran

...more of

WE'RE #1, WE'RE #1

"Keep on Loving You"
REO Speedwagon

"Rapture"
Blondie

"Kiss on My List"
Daryl Hall and John Oates

"Morning Train (Nine to Five)"
Sheena Easton

"Bette Davis Eyes"
Kim Carnes

"Stars on 45"
Stars on 45

"The One That You Love"
Air Supply

"Jessie's Girl"
Rick Springfield

"Endless Love"
Diana Ross and Lionel Richie

"Arthur's Theme (Best That You Can Do)"
Christopher Cross

"Private Eyes"
Daryl Hall and John Oates

"Physical"
Olivia Newton-John

GO ON TO THE NEXT PAGE

 GO ON TO THE NEXT PAGE

. . . more of

1982

"I Can't Go for That (No Can Do)"
Daryl Hall and John Oates

"Centerfold"
The J. Geils Band

"I Love Rock 'n Roll"
Joan Jett and the Blackhearts

"Chariots of Fire — Titles"
Vangelis

"Ebony and Ivory"
Paul McCartney with Stevie Wonder

"Don't You Want Me"
The Human League

"Eye of the Tiger"
Survivor

"Abracadabra"
The Steve Miller Band

"Hard to Say I'm Sorry"
Chicago

"Jack and Diane"
John Cougar

"Who Can It Be Now?"
Men at Work

"Up Where We Belong"
Joe Cocker and Jennifer Warnes

117. **Legends at Live Aid**

    (A) Joan Baez
    (B) Robert Plant
    (C) Bob Dylan
    (D) Johnny Cash
    (E) Paul McCartney

118. **Americans at Live Aid**

    (A) Madonna
    (B) Huey Lewis and the News
    (C) Run-D.M.C.
    (D) The Hooters
    (E) Kenny Loggins

119. **Motown in USA for Africa**

    (A) Smokey Robinson
    (B) Diana Ross
    (C) Dan Aykroyd
    (D) Ray Charles
    (E) James Brown

120. **Country in USA for Africa**

    (A) Waylon Jennings
    (B) Willie Nelson
    (C) Kenny Rogers
    (D) Dolly Parton
    (E) Bruce Springsteen

121. **Jacksons in USA for Africa**

    (A) Jackie Jackson
    (B) Tito Jackson
    (C) Janet Jackson
    (D) La Toya Jackson
    (E) Marlon Jackson

122. **Not in USA for Africa**

    (A) Prince
    (B) Sheila E.
    (C) Madonna
    (D) Pat Benatar
    (E) Donna Summer

GO ON TO THE NEXT PAGE

GO ON TO THE NEXT PAGE

Questions 123–130 refer to alternative music.

123. Songs by R.E.M.

   (A) "Talk About the Passion"
   (B) "Take the Skinheads Bowling"
   (C) "Superman"
   (D) "Orange Crush"
   (E) "Fall on Me"

124. Songs by The Smiths

   (A) "Bigmouth Strikes Again"
   (B) "Frankly, Mr. Shankly"
   (C) "How Soon Is Now?"
   (D) "Heaven Knows I'm Miserable Now"
   (E) "Everyday Is Like Sunday"

125. Songs by The Cure

   (A) "Lullaby"
   (B) "Just Like Heaven"
   (C) "Close to You"
   (D) "Let's Go to Bed"
   (E) "Killing an Arab"

126. Songs by New Order

   (A) "Love Vigilantes"
   (B) "Love My Way"
   (C) "Bizarre Love Triangle"
   (D) "Perfect Kiss"
   (E) "Confusion"

127. Songs by Depeche Mode

   (A) "People Are People"
   (B) "Strangelove"
   (C) "Everything Counts"
   (D) "Just Can't Get Enough"
   (E) "Who Needs Love Like That"

. . . more of
WE'RE #1, WE'RE #1

"Truly"
Lionel Richie

"Mickey"
Toni Basil

"Maneater"
Daryl Hall and John Oates

1983

"Down Under"
Men at Work

"Africa"
Toto

"Baby, Come to Me"
Patti Austin with James Ingram

"Billie Jean"
Michael Jackson

"Come On Eileen"
Dexy's Midnight Runners

"Beat It"
Michael Jackson

"Let's Dance"
David Bowie

"Flashdance . . . What a Feeling"
Irene Cara

"Every Breath You Take"
The Police

GO ON TO THE NEXT PAGE

GO ON TO THE NEXT PAGE

... more of

WE'RE #1, WE'RE #1!

"Sweet Dreams (Are Made of This)"
Eurythmics

"Maniac"
Michael Sembello

"Tell Her About It"
Billie Joel

"Total Eclipse of the Heart"
Bonnie Tyler

"Islands in the Stream"
Kenny Rogers and Dolly Parton

"All Night Long (All Night)"
Lionel Richie

"Say Say Say"
Paul McCartney and Michael Jackson

1984

"Owner of a Lonely Heart"
Yes

"Karma Chameleon"
Culture Club

"Jump"
Van Halen

"Footloose"
Kenny Loggins

"Against All Odds (Take a Look at Me Now)"
Phil Collins

GO ON TO THE NEXT PAGE

128. **Real musicians names**

    (A)   Siouxsie Sioux
    (B)   Black Francis
    (C)   Jello Biafra
    (D)   Iron Sheik
    (E)   Budgie

129. **Real band names**

    (A)   Happy Mondays
    (B)   Hüsker Dü
    (C)   Front 242
    (D)   Tones on Tail
    (E)   The Placemats

130. **More real band names**

    (A)   Black Flag
    (B)   Komodo Dragon
    (C)   The Dead Kennedys
    (D)   Meat Puppets
    (E)   Dead Milkmen

GO ON TO THE NEXT PAGE

131. Members of U2

(A) Paul Hewson
(B) Daniel Evans
(C) Larry Mullen, Jr.
(D) Adam Clayton
(E) The Edge

132. Members of The Go-Go's

(A) Kathy Valentine
(B) Gina Schock
(C) Belinda Carlisle
(D) Janet Wiedlin
(E) Charlotte Caffey

133. Members of The Bangles

(A) Michael Steele
(B) Susanna Hoffs
(C) Vicki Peterson
(D) Debbi Peterson
(E) Michelle Irons

134. Members of New Kids on the Block

(A) Mark Wahlberg
(B) Jordan Knight
(C) Joe McIntyre
(D) Danny Wood
(E) Jonathan Knight

135. Members of New Edition

(A) Ralph Tresvant
(B) Michael Bivins
(C) Ricky Bell
(D) Ronnie DeVoe
(E) Kendall Gill

... more of
WE'RE #1, WE'RE #1

"Hello"
Lionel Richie

"Let's Hear It for the Boy"
Deniece Williams

"Time After Time"
Cyndi Lauper

"The Reflex"
Duran Duran

"When Doves Cry"
Prince and the Revolution

"Ghostbusters"
Ray Parker Jr.

"What's Love Got to Do with It"
Tina Turner

"Missing You"
John Waite

"Let's Go Crazy"
Prince and the Revolution

"I Just Called to Say I Love You"
Stevie Wonder

"Carribean Queen (No More Love on the Run)"
Billy Ocean

"Wake Me Up Before You Go-Go"
Wham!

"Out of Touch"
Daryl Hall and John Oates

GO ON TO THE NEXT PAGE

GO ON TO THE NEXT PAGE

. . . more of
WE'RE #1, WE'RE #1!

"Like a Virgin"
Madonna

1985

"I Want to Know What Love Is"
Foreigner

"Careless Whisper"
Wham! featuring George Michael

"Can't Fight This Feeling"
REO Speedwagon

"One More Night"
Phil Collins

"We Are the World"
USA for Africa

"Crazy for You"
Madonna

"Don't You (Forget About Me)"
Simple Minds

"Everything She Wants"
Wham!

"Everybody Wants to Rule the World"
Tears for Fears

"Heaven"
Bryan Adams

"Sussudio"
Phil Collins

Musical analogies

Directions: The following questions contain a pair of music-related items and the first part of a second pair of music-related items. Select the lettered answer that best expresses a relationship similar to that expressed in the original pair.

Questions 136–145 refer to **soundtracks.**

136. "Don't You (Forget About Me)" : *The Breakfast Club* :: "If You Leave" :

    (A) *Pretty in Pink*
    (B) *The Breakfast Club*
    (C) *Weird Science*
    (D) *St. Elmo's Fire*
    (E) *Sixteen Candles*

137. "The Power of Love" : *Back to the Future* :: "I'm Alright" :

    (A) *Gremlins*
    (B) *Caddyshack*
    (C) *The Lost Boys*
    (D) *Rocky II*
    (E) *Top Gun*

138. "Let's Hear It for the Boy" : *Footloose* :: "I'm Free (Heaven Helps the Man)" :

    (A) *Footloose*
    (B) *Flashdance*
    (C) *Dirty Dancing*
    (D) *Streets of Fire*
    (E) *Top Gun*

GO ON TO THE NEXT PAGE

GO ON TO THE NEXT PAGE

139. "Maniac" : *Flashdance* :: "New Attitude" :

   (A) *Beverly Hills Cop*
   (B) *Big*
   (C) *The Pick-Up Artist*
   (D) *Footloose*
   (E) *Tootsie*

140. "Almost Paradise" : *Footloose* :: "Crazy for You" :

   (A) *Purple Rain*
   (B) *Vision Quest*
   (C) *Who's That Girl?*
   (D) *Desperately Seeking Susan*
   (E) *Quicksilver*

141. "Take My Breath Away" : *Top Gun* :: "You Belong to the City" :

   (A) *Miami Vice*
   (B) *Beverly Hills Cop II*
   (C) *Beverly Hills Cop*
   (D) *Less Than Zero*
   (E) *Moonlighting*

142. "Into the Groove" : *Desperately Seeking Susan* :: "Hazy Shade of Winter" :

   (A) *Top Gun*
   (B) *The Lost Boys*
   (C) *Less Than Zero*
   (D) *About Last Night…*
   (E) *Do the Right Thing*

143. "Old Time Rock & Roll" : *Risky Business* :: "Neutron Dance" :

   (A) *Footloose*
   (B) *Beverly Hills Cop*
   (C) *Valley Girl*
   (D) *Midnight Run*
   (E) *48 HRS.*

. . . more of
WE'RE #1, WE'RE #1

"A View to a Kill"
Duran Duran

"Everytime You Go Away"
Paul Young

"Shout"
Tears for Fears

"The Power of Love"
Huey Lewis and the News

"St. Elmo's Fire (Man in Motion)"
John Parr

"Money for Nothing"
Dire Straits

"Oh Sheila"
Ready for the World

"Take on Me"
a-ha

"Saving All My Love for You"
Whitney Houston

"Part-Time Lover"
Stevie Wonder

"Miami Vice Theme"
Jan Hammer

"We Built This City"
Starship

"Separate Lives"
Phil Collins and Marilyn Martin

GO ON TO THE NEXT PAGE

GO ON TO THE NEXT PAGE

. . . more of

"Broken Wings"
Mr. Mister

"Say You, Say Me"
Lionel Richie

1986

"That's What Friends Are For"
Dionne & Friends

"How Will I Know"
Whitney Houston

"Kyrie"
Mr. Mister

"Sara"
Starship

"These Dreams"
Heart

"Rock Me Amadeus"
Falco

"Kiss"
Prince and the Revolution

"Addicted to Love"
Robert Palmer

"West End Girls"
Pet Shop Boys

"Greatest Love of All"
Whitney Houston

GO ON TO THE NEXT PAGE

144. "(I've Had) The Time of My Life" : *Dirty Dancing* :: "I Do What I Do" :

   (A) *Miami Vice*
   (B) *Rumble Fish*
   (C) *Body Heat*
   (D) *A View to a Kill*
   (E) *9½ Weeks*

145. "She's Like the Wind" : *Dirty Dancing* :: "Somebody's Baby Tonight" :

   (A) *Miami Vice*
   (B) *Valley Girl*
   (C) *Dirty Dancing*
   (D) *Fast Times at Ridgemont High*
   (E) *Legal Eagles*

Questions 146–155 refer to albums.

146. "Africa" : *Toto IV* :: "Panama" :

   (A) *Skyscraper*
   (B) *Fair Warning*
   (C) *Diver Down*
   (D) *5150*
   (E) *1984*

147. "Eyes Without a Face" : *Rebel Yell* :: "Devil Inside" :

   (A) *Bummed*
   (B) *Shabooh Shoobah*
   (C) *Kick*
   (D) *Zenyatta Mondatta*
   (E) *Listen Like Thieves*

148. "No Reply at All" : *Abacab* :: "Don't Lose My Number" :

   (A) *Invisible Touch*
   (B) *. . . But Seriously*
   (C) *Face Value*
   (D) *No Jacket Required*
   (E) *Pretzel Logic*

GO ON TO THE NEXT PAGE

149. "Overkill" : *Cargo* :: "Heart and Soul" :

   (A) *1999*
   (B) *Picture This*
   (C) *Fore!*
   (D) *Sports*
   (E) *T'Pau's Greatest Hits*

150. "P.Y.T. (Pretty Young Thing)" : *Thriller* :: "U Got the Look" :

   (A) *Alphabet City*
   (B) *A Private Heaven*
   (C) *Lovesexy*
   (D) *Around the World in a Day*
   (E) *Sign 'O' the Times*

151. "Uptown Girl" : *An Innocent Man* :: "Material Girl" :

   (A) *Madonna*
   (B) *True Blue*
   (C) *Like a Virgin*
   (D) *Like a Prayer*
   (E) *Who's That Girl*

152. "Shout" : *Songs From the Big Chair* :: "New Moon on Monday" :

   (A) *Rio*
   (B) *Seven and the Ragged Tiger*
   (C) *Duran Duran*
   (D) *Big Thing*
   (E) *Different Light*

153. "Good Thing" : *The Raw and the Cooked* :: "Bad" :

   (A) *Girl You Know It's True*
   (B) *The Unforgettable Fire*
   (C) *War*
   (D) *New Jersey*
   (E) *Dangerous*

. . . more of
WE'RE #1, WE'RE #1

"Live to Tell"
Madonna

"On My Own"
Patti LaBelle and Michael McDonald

"There'll Be Sad Songs (To Make You Cry)"
Billy Ocean

"Holding Back the Years"
Simply Red

"Invisible Touch"
Genesis

"Sledgehammer"
Peter Gabriel

"Glory of Love"
Peter Cetera

"Papa Don't Preach"
Madonna

"Higher Love"
Steve Winwood

"Venus"
Bananarama

"Take My Breath Away"
Berlin

"Stuck with You"
Huey Lewis and the News

"When I Think of You"
Janet Jackson

GO ON TO THE NEXT PAGE

GO ON TO THE NEXT PAGE

... more of

WE'RE #1, WE'RE #1!

"True Colors"
Cyndi Lauper

"Amanda"
Boston

"Human"
The Human League

"You Give Love a Bad Name"
Bon Jovi

"The Next Time I Fall"
Peter Cetera with Amy Grant

"The Way It Is"
Bruce Hornsby & the Range

"Walk Like an Egyptian"
The Bangles

1987

"Shake You Down"
Gregory Abbott

"At This Moment"
Billy Vera & the Beaters

"Open Your Heart"
Madonna

"Livin' on a Prayer"
Bon Jovi

"Jacob's Ladder"
Huey Lewis and the News

154. "Shock the Monkey" : *Security* :: "Monkey Gone to Heaven" :

(A) *Surfer Rosa*
(B) *The Queen Is Dead*
(C) *The Blow Monkeys*
(D) *Dirk Wears White Sox*
(E) *Doolittle*

155. "Pink Cadillac" : *Born in the U.S.A.* :: "Pink Houses" :

(A) *Uh-huh*
(B) *American Fool*
(C) *Brothers in Arms*
(D) *Scarecrow*
(E) *Who's Zoomin' Who*

Questions 156–165 refer to **foreigners.**

156. Falco : Vienna :: Rush :

(A) Edmonton
(B) Ottawa
(C) Toronto
(D) Montreal
(E) Vancouver

157. INXS : Australia :: Sheena Easton :

(A) Ireland
(B) Australia
(C) Canada
(D) England
(E) Scotland

158. Genesis : England :: Dire Straits :

(A) England
(B) Ireland
(C) Canada
(D) Germany
(E) New Zealand

 GO ON TO THE NEXT PAGE

159. Scorpions : Germany :: a-ha :

- (A) Sweden
- (B) Norway
- (C) Denmark
- (D) Finland
- (E) Switzerland

160. U2 : Ireland :: Sade :

- (A) Nigeria
- (B) England
- (C) France
- (D) Chad
- (E) Qatar

Questions 161–165 refer to Americans.

161. Prince : Minneapolis :: Michael Jackson :

- (A) Chicago
- (B) Detroit
- (C) Nashville
- (D) Gary, Indiana
- (E) Milwaukee

162. Bon Jovi : New Jersey :: ZZ Top :

- (A) California
- (B) Louisiana
- (C) Missouri
- (D) Nevada
- (E) Texas

163. Whitney Houston : Newark, New Jersey :: Cyndi Lauper :

- (A) New Brunswick, New Jersey
- (B) Brooklyn, New York
- (C) Queens, New York
- (D) New York, New York
- (E) Boston, Massachusetts

. . . more of
WE'RE #1, WE'RE #1

"Lean on Me"
Club Nouveau

"Nothing's Gonna Stop Us Now"
Starship

"I Knew You Were Waiting (for Me)"
Aretha Franklin and George Michael

"(I Just) Died in Your Arms"
Cutting Crew

"With or Without You"
U2

"You Keep Me Hangin' On"
Kim Wilde

"Always"
Atlantic Starr

"Head to Toe"
Lisa Lisa and Cult Jam

"I Wanna Dance with Somebody (Who Loves Me)"
Whitney Houston

"Alone"
Heart

"Shakedown"
Bob Seger

"I Still Haven't Found What I'm Looking For"
U2

"Who's That Girl"
Madonna

GO ON TO THE NEXT PAGE

GO ON TO THE NEXT PAGE

. . . more of

WE'RE #1, WE'RE #1!

"La Bamba"
Los Lobos

"I Just Can't Stop Loving You"
Michael Jackson

"Didn't We Almost Have It All"
Whitney Houston

"Here I Go Again"
Whitesnake

"Lost in Emotion"
Lisa Lisa and Cult Jam

"Bad"
Michael Jackson

"I Think We're Alone Now"
Tiffany

"Mony Mony 'Live'"
Billy Idol

"(I've Had) The Time of My Life"
Bill Medley and Jennifer Warnes

"Heaven Is a Place on Earth"
Belinda Carlisle

"Faith"
George Michael

1988

"So Emotional"
Whitney Houston

164. Daryl Hall : Pennsylvania :: John Cougar Mellencamp :

(A) Iowa
(B) Indiana
(C) Illinois
(D) Kansas
(E) Nebraska

165. Madonna : Bay City, Michigan :: Heart :

(A) Los Angeles
(B) San Francisco
(C) Seattle
(D) Oakland
(E) San Diego

GO ON TO THE NEXT PAGE

GO ON TO THE NEXT PAGE

Whose power ballad are you?

Below are two groups of five questions, each question consisting of a wimpy song by a hard rock band (Column A) and a hard rock band (Column B). In each group, you are to match the power ballad in Column A to the band in Column B that performed it. If you get stuck, holding up your lighter might help. (Note: Each band in Column B will be chosen only once per group.)

Group 1

A   **B**

166. "Is This Love"   (A) Def Leppard
167. "Still Loving You"   (B) Guns N' Roses
168. "Love Bites"   (C) Scorpions
169. "When the Children Cry"   (D) White Lion
170. "Sweet Child o' Mine"   (E) Whitesnake

Group 2

A   **B**

171. "Every Rose Has Its Thorn"   (A) Bon Jovi
172. "When It's Love"   (B) Lita Ford (with Ozzy Osbourne)
173. "Wanted Dead or Alive"   (C) Mötley Crüe
174. "Home Sweet Home"   (D) Poison
175. "Close My Eyes Forever"   (E) Van Halen

. . . more of
WE'RE #1, WE'RE #1

"Got My Mind Set on You"
George Harrison

"The Way You Make Me Feel"
Michael Jackson

"Need You Tonight"
INXS

"Could've Been"
Tiffany

"Seasons Change"
Exposé

"Father Figure"
George Michael

"Never Gonna Give You Up"
Rick Astley

"Man in the Mirror"
Michael Jackson

"Get Outta My Dreams, Get into My Car"
Billy Ocean

"Where Do Broken Hearts Go"
Whitney Houston

"Wishing Well"
Terence Trent D'Arby

"Anything for You"
Gloria Estefan and Miami Sound Machine

"One More Try"
George Michael

GO ON TO THE NEXT PAGE

GO ON TO THE NEXT PAGE

... more of

WE'RE #1, WE'RE #1!

"Together Forever"
Rick Astley

"Foolish Beat"
Debbie Gibson

"Dirty Diana"
Michael Jackson

"The Flame"
Cheap Trick

"Hold On to the Nights"
Richard Marx

"Roll with It"
Steve Winwood

"Monkey"
George Michael

"Sweet Child o' Mine"
Guns N' Roses

"Don't Worry Be Happy"
Bobby McFerrin

"Love Bites"
Def Leppard

"Red Red Wine"
UB40

"Groovy Kind of Love"
Phil Collins

"Kokomo"
The Beach Boys

Fill In the blanks

Directions: Each sentence below has one or two blanks, each blank indicating that something has been omitted. Beneath the sentence are five lettered items or sets of items. Choose the answer for each blank that best fits the meaning of the sentence as a whole.

**Questions 176–180 refer to
big-hair bands.**

Big hair and rock 'n' roll seemed merged at the spandex-covered hip in the '80s. In each question below, fill in the blank or blanks relating to pop-metal and heavy-metal bands.

176. When ——— left the biggest rock group of the '80s in 1985, fans cried foul; he later had a big hit with the Steve Vai–inspired "Yankee Rose."

(A) Gene Simmons
(B) Ted Nugent
(C) Ozzie Osbourne
(D) Jon Bon Jovi
(E) David Lee Roth

177. The goony-looking ——— fronted Twisted Sister, whose borderline joke song, ——— , was an MTV smash in 1984.

(A) Vince Neil; "Looks That Kill"
(B) David Coverdale; "Still of the Night"
(C) Sammy Hagar; "I Can't Drive 55"
(D) Dee Snider; "We're Not Gonna Take It"
(E) Don Dokken; "I Wanna Rock"

GO ON TO THE NEXT PAGE

178. Poison covered their makeup-encrusted predecessors Kiss with ——— in 1988, while ——— took on Slade's "Cum On Feel the Noize" five years earlier.

(A) "Rock and Roll All Nite"; Quiet Riot
(B) "Detroit City Blues"; Kiss
(C) "Smokin' in the Boys Room"; Van Halen
(D) "Beth"; Ratt
(E) "Bohemian Rhapsody"; Scorpions

179. In 1988, hard-rockin', hard-boozin' ——— scored big with its ballad "Sweet Child o' Mine"; four years earlier, mall rockers ——— shopped around "Sister Christian."

(A) Skid Row; Van Halen
(B) Guns N' Roses; Night Ranger
(C) Slaughter; Night Ranger
(D) Guns N' Roses; Bon Jovi
(E) George Thorogood and the Destroyers; Cinderella

180. Early imprisonment was the sad tale in ———'s "18 and Life," while pedophilia (a jailable offense) reared its ugly head in "Seventeen" by ——— .

(A) White Lion; Aerosmith
(B) Great White; Paul Hardcastle
(C) Skid Row; Winger
(D) Damn Yankees; Warrant
(E) Nelson; Winger

. . . more of

"Wild, Wild West"
The Escape Club

"Bad Medicine"
Bon Jovi

"Baby, I Love Your Way/ Freedbird Medley (Free Baby)"
Will to Power

"Look Away"
Chicago

"Every Rose Has Its Thorn"
Poison

1989

"My Prerogative"
Bobby Brown

"Two Hearts"
Phil Collins

"When I'm with You"
Sheriff

"Straight Up"
Paula Abdul

"Lost in Your Eyes"
Debbie Gibson

"The Living Years"
Mike + the Mechanics

"Eternal Flame"
The Bangles

GO ON TO THE NEXT PAGE

GO ON TO THE NEXT PAGE

. . . more of

WE'RE #1, WE'RE #1!

"The Look"
Roxette

"She Drives Me Crazy"
Fine Young Cannibals

"Like a Prayer"
Madonna

"I'll Be There for You"
Bon Jovi

"Forever Your Girl"
Paula Abdul

"Rock On"
Michael Damian

"Wind Beneath My Wings"
Bette Midler

"I'll Be Loving You (Forever)"
New Kids on the Block

"Satisfied"
Richard Marx

"Baby Don't Forget My Number"
Milli Vanilli

"Good Thing"
Fine Young Cannibals

"If You Don't Know Me by Now"
Simply Red

"Toy Soldiers"
Martika

Questions 181–190 refer to
one-hit wonders.

No other decade spawned as many successful failures as the big '80s. In each question below, fill in the blank or blanks relating to one-hit wonders.

181. Not-so-pretty-boys ———— hit #1 while pleading "Come On Eileen."

(A) A Flock of Seagulls
(B) Pretty Poison
(C) Sigue Sigue Sputnik
(D) Kajagoogoo
(E) Dexy's Midnight Runners

182. "Keep Your Hands to Yourself" were the famous last words by ———— .

(A) Georgia Satellites
(B) Timbuk 3
(C) Go West
(D) Kajagoogoo
(E) Chilliwack

183. The video for Bobby McFerrin's "Don't Worry Be Happy" starred ———— .

(A) Dr. Ruth
(B) Nathan Lane
(C) Chevy Chase
(D) Robin Williams
(E) Rae Dawn Chong

184. The group responsible for the novelty song "Pac-Man Fever" was ———— ; the ultra-weird "Fish Heads" was arranged by ———— .

(A) Boys Don't Cry; Prince
(B) Joe Dolce Music Theatre; Herbie Hancock
(C) Japan; Wall of Voodoo
(D) Weird Al Yankovic; Devo
(E) Buckner & Garcia; Barnes & Barnes

GO ON TO THE NEXT PAGE

GO ON TO THE NEXT PAGE

185. The English band ——— took Falco's "Der Kommissar" to #5 in 1983; a year later, the English version of ———'s "99 Luftballons" floated to #2.

   (A) Spandau Ballet; Taco
   (B) After the Fire; Falco
   (C) Modern English; Peter Schilling
   (D) The Blow Monkeys; Nena
   (E) After the Fire; Nena

186. Both Don Johnson (*Miami Vice*) and Bruce Willis (*Moonlighting*) traded on their television success to hit #5 with their respective songs, ——— and ——— .

   (A) "Smuggler's Blues"; "Bruno's Bop"
   (B) "Heartbreaker"; "Under the Boardwalk"
   (C) "All I Need"; "It's Now or Never"
   (D) "Heartbeat"; "Respect Yourself"
   (E) "Holding Out for a Hero"; "Secret Agent Man"

187. Matthew Wilder's only hit was the giddy ——— , while Scritti Politti's lone witty ditty was ——— .

   (A) "Never Gonna Give You Up"; "Don't Go"
   (B) "Break My Stride"; "Perfect Way"
   (C) "Tarzan Boy"; "Take On Me"
   (D) "We Don't Have to Take Our Clothes Off"; "In a Big Country"
   (E) "The Politics of Dancing"; "Mony Mony"

188. ———'s "One Night in Bangkok" was his one-hit stand; ——— tried to "Pass the Dutchie" but was never heard from again.

   (A) Murray Head; Musical Youth
   (B) Peter Schilling; Menudo
   (C) Tommy Tutone; Toni Basil
   (D) Taco; Musical Youth
   (E) Gary Numan; Nu Shooz

. . . *more of*
WE'RE #1, WE'RE #1

"Batdance"
Prince

"Right Here Waiting"
Richard Marx

"Cold Hearted"
Paula Abdul

"Hangin' Tough"
New Kids on the Block

"Don't Wanna Lose You"
Gloria Estefan

"Girl I'm Gonna Miss You"
Milli Vanilli

"Miss You Much"
Janet Jackson

"Listen to Your Heart"
Roxette

"When I See You Smile"
Bad English

"Blame It on the Rain"
Milli Vanilli

"We Didn't Start the Fire"
Billy Joel

"Another Day in Paradise"
Phil Collins

GO ON TO THE NEXT PAGE

189. Sly's bro Frank Stallone made it to only #10 with ——— , from the movie *Staying Alive;* Sly Fox's ——— (#7) also didn't stay alive long enough to hit the top spot.

(A) "I Can't Hold Back"; "Don't Forget Me (When I'm Gone)"

(B) "Far From Over"; "Let's Go All the Way"

(C) "Eye of the Tiger"; "One Thing Leads to Another"

(D) "Never Surrender"; "The Night Owls"

(E) "Midnight Blue"; "A Girl in Trouble (Is a Temporary Thing)"

190. The diminutive ——— was all over MTV with "Fantasy"; Spandau Ballet's ballad ——— even cracked the Top Ten.

(A) Oran "Juice" Jones; "No New Tale To Tell"

(B) Regina; "True"

(C) Aldo Nova; "True"

(D) Stacey Q; "Avalon"

(E) Shannon; "More Than This"

Questions 191–200 refer to rap.

Though rap has its origins in the '70s, the genre hit its strut in the '80s. In each question below, fill in the blank or blanks relating to rap music.

191. Run-D.M.C.'s DJ was ——— .

(A) Terminator X

(B) Melle Mel

(C) Jam Master Jay

(D) Spinderella

(E) Mix-master Ice

192. The old-school trio ——— had a big hit with "Freaks Come Out at Night," and they later wrote a song called "I'm a Ho."

(A) Grandmaster Flash

(B) U.T.F.O.

(C) The Geto Boys

(D) Whodini

(E) The Fat Boys

193. Rap label Def Jam's inaugural release was the first album by ——— .

(A) Run-D.M.C.

(B) The Beastie Boys

(C) L. L. Cool J

(D) Big Daddy Kane

(E) De La Soul

194. The first album by DJ Jazzy Jeff & the Fresh Prince was ——— .

(A) *Rock the House*

(B) *King of Rock*

(C) *He's the DJ, I'm the Rapper*

(D) *Yo! Bum Rush the Show*

(E) *Raise the Roof*

Oddville, MTV

Five really weird videos of the 1980s:

Rockit, Herbie Hancock (1983)

There wasn't a plot to the Rockit video — just a rack of dancing clothes, a pair of mechanized mannequin legs going in circles around a room, and a metallic guy getting his head pushed repeatedly into a bowl of cereal. Cool "scratching" and synth music, though.

Through Being Cool, Devo (1982)

This video had the boys from Akron, Ohio, playing with ray guns. The quintet ran around and eliminated all the "ninnies and the twirps," such as yuppie joggers and locker-room bullies. The low-budget special effects and the goofy facial reactions of their victims were pretty strange, but I guess for the flowerpot-wearing Devo it wasn't that weird.

Mexican Radio, Wall of Voodoo (1982)

At the end of this video, which showcases the song with the lyric "I wish I was in Tijuana / eating barbecued iguana," a guy sticks his face up through a drum filled with refried beans. Truly disturbing.

Once in a Lifetime, Talking Heads (1980)

With a waterlike backdrop, this funky video saw David Byrne contorting his body and creating a new dance by bouncing his hand along his forearm. Brilliantly crazy.

Hello, Lionel Richie (1984)

Come on! Along with featuring the line "All I know is this and the can" delivered by a guy in a drama class, this video about a much older teacher (Richie) stalking a cute blind student was actionable. Plus he rhymes "hello," with "for." Weird.

Talking Heads

GO ON TO THE NEXT PAGE

195. Two of the most popular rap songs of the
'80s included "Bust a Move" by ——— and
"Funky Cold Medina" by ——— .

(A) Grandmaster Flash and the Furious
Five; The Fat Boys
(B) P.M. Dawn; KRS-One
(C) Young MC; Tone Lōc
(D) Vanilla Ice; Tone Lōc
(E) Young MC; Young MC

196. "It's just too bad that girl's a bum" were lyrics
by ——— ; "Sophisticated Bitch" was a song
off the first album by ——— .

(A) Kurtis Blow; U.T.F.O.
(B) The Beastie Boys; Public Enemy
(C) The Beastie Boys; 2 Live Crew
(D) KRS-One; De La Soul
(E) Biz Markee; N.W.A.

197. Hard-rockin' Aerosmith strutted with ———
for a rap version of "Walk This Way," while
the heavy metal band Anthrax laid down a
hard groove on the album *Lethal* by ——— .

(A) Run-D.M.C.; Ice-T
(B) The Beastie Boys; Vanilla Ice
(C) Run-D.M.C.; Public Enemy
(D) Tone Lōc; Ice Cube
(E) Run-D.M.C.; U.T.F.O.

198. Female rappers include ——— , who recorded "Push It," and ——— , who first hit the
scene in 1988 with "I Cram to Understand U
(Sam)."

(A) Salt-n-Pepa; Sheila E.
(B) Salt-n-Pepa; MC Lyte
(C) MC Lyte; Roxanne Shanté
(D) Salt-n-Pepa; Roxanne Shanté
(E) Sheila E.; Salt-n-Pepa

199. "Go See the Doctor" was rapped by ——— ;
the rapper on Chaka Khan's "I Feel For You"
was ——— .

(A) Tone Lōc; Run-D.M.C.
(B) The Fresh Prince; Grandmaster Flash
(C) Kool Moe Dee; Melle Mel
(D) Tone Lōc; Kool Moe Dee
(E) Doug E. Fresh; Kurtis Blow

200. Both ——— and ——— were in the 1985
rap movie *Krush Groove*.

(A) Kurtis Blow; The Fat Boys
(B) The Beastie Boys; Salt-n-Pepa
(C) Run-D.M.C.; Kool Moe Dee
(D) Sir Mix-a-Lot; Kurtis Blow
(E) L. L. Cool J; Heavy D.

STOP!

You have reached the End of Section III

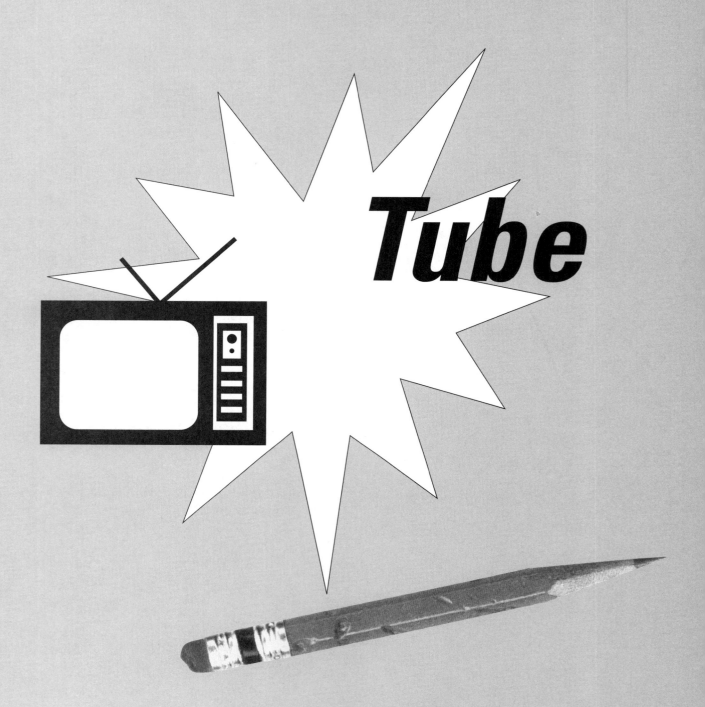

Theme song multiple choice

Directions: Each question below contains some lyrics from a TV theme song, followed by five lettered shows. Choose the show that best matches the lyrics.

1. "Just-ah good ol' boys, never meanin' no harm . . ."

   (A) *Riptide*
   (B) *What's Happening Now!!*
   (C) *The Dukes of Hazzard*
   (D) *Bosom Buddies*
   (E) *Simon & Simon*

2. "Believe it or not, it's just me . . ."

   (A) *Hooperman*
   (B) *The Greatest American Hero*
   (C) *Manimal*
   (D) *Angie*
   (E) *Silver Spoons*

3. "Then along come two, they got nothing but their dreams . . ."

   (A) *Mork & Mindy*
   (B) *The Blue Falcon and Dynomutt Show*
   (C) *Diff'rent Strokes*
   (D) *Webster*
   (E) *Double Trouble*

4. "when the world never seems to be living up to your dreams"

   (A) *Diff'rent Strokes*
   (B) *One Day at a Time*
   (C) *It's Your Move*
   (D) *Angie*
   (E) *The Facts of Life*

5. "Making your way in the world today takes everything you got . . ."

   (A) *Family Ties*
   (B) *The Cosby Show*
   (C) *Miami Vice*
   (D) *Cheers*
   (E) *Punky Brewster*

GO ON TO THE NEXT PAGE

6. "There's a new girl in town and she's feelin' good . . ."

   (A) *Flo*
   (B) *Small Wonder*
   (C) *Punky Brewster*
   (D) *Oh Madeline*
   (E) *Alice*

7. "let it flow, it flows back to you"

   (A) *Fast Times*
   (B) *The Love Boat*
   (C) *Hart to Hart*
   (D) *Square Pegs*
   (E) *Moonlighting*

8. "Now I never spent much time in school, but I've taught ladies plenty . . ."

   (A) *MacGyver*
   (B) *Matlock*
   (C) *Tales of the Gold Monkey*
   (D) *Doogie Howser, M.D.*
   (E) *The Fall Guy*

9. "There's a road you take and a road not taken . . ."

   (A) *Knight Rider*
   (B) *Who's the Boss?*
   (C) *Just the Ten of Us*
   (D) *Growing Pains*
   (E) *The Highwayman*

Mork and Mindy

GO ON TO THE NEXT PAGE

10. "New dreams and a fine machine, but best of all I don't pay property tax . . ."

   (A) *B.J. and the Bear*
   (B) *Convoy*
   (C) *Automan*
   (D) *a.k.a. Pablo*
   (E) *Hardcastle and McCormick*

11. "I'm tired of pretendin', I want a happy endin', won't let 'em get the best of me . . ."

   (A) *The Powers of Matthew Star*
   (B) *Mr. Merlin*
   (C) *Square Pegs*
   (D) *Gimme a Break*
   (E) *One Day at a Time*

12. "La, la, la-la, la, la, sing a happy song . . ."

   (A) *Beauty and the Beast*
   (B) *Snorks*
   (C) *The Littles*
   (D) *Monchhichis*
   (E) *Smurfs*

13. "Fish don't fry in the kitchen, beans don't burn on the grill . . ."

   (A) *Checking In*
   (B) *227*
   (C) *The Jeffersons*
   (D) *Wok with Yan*
   (E) *Three's a Crowd*

14. "Maybe the world is blind, or just a little unkind. Don't know."

   (A) *The Golden Girls*
   (B) *Sledge Hammer!*
   (C) *Punky Brewster*
   (D) *Women in Prison*
   (E) *Amen*

15. "Together, we're gonna find our way . . ."

   (A) *Silver Spoons*
   (B) *Punky Brewster*
   (C) *Perfect Strangers*
   (D) *It's Your Move*
   (E) *Joanie Loves Chachi*

16. "Show me that smile again . . ."

   (A) *The Famous Teddy Z*
   (B) *Double Trouble*
   (C) *Who's the Boss?*
   (D) *Punky Brewster*
   (E) *Growing Pains*

17. "You'll find you need us 'cause there's no one else to call . . ."

   (A) *21 Jump Street*
   (B) *The Real Ghostbusters*
   (C) *The Facts of Life*
   (D) *The Bloodhound Gang*
   (E) *The A-Team*

18. "This is it, this is life, the one you get, so go and have a ball . . ."

   (A) *One Day at a Time*
   (B) *The Brady Brides*
   (C) *Full House*
   (D) *Life Goes On*
   (E) *It's a Living*

19. "Streaks on the china never mattered before. Who cares?"

   (A) *Benson*
   (B) *Designing Women*
   (C) *Valerie*
   (D) *Mr. Belvedere*
   (E) *Charles in Charge*

GO ON TO THE NEXT PAGE

20. "We've a lovable space that needs your face . . ."

(A) *American Bandstand*
(B) *Laverne and Shirley*
(C) *Fame*
(D) *Too Close for Comfort*
(E) *Three's Company*

21. "Sha-la-la-la."

(A) *Sha Na Na*
(B) *Family Ties*
(C) *The Wonder Years*
(D) *Moonlighting*
(E) *Smurfs*

22. "life goes on, right or wrong"

(A) *Dear John*
(B) *Life Goes On*
(C) *The Wonder Years*
(D) *Duet*
(E) *The Tortellis*

23. "Thank you for being a friend . . ."

(A) *Here's Boomer*
(B) *The Golden Girls*
(C) *Designing Women*
(D) *Perfect Strangers*
(E) *ALF*

24. "it's my life, my dream — nothing's gonna stop me now"

(A) *9 to 5*
(B) *The Greatest American Hero*
(C) *Perfect Strangers*
(D) *It's a Living*
(E) *Three's a Crowd*

25. "You can count on me no matter what you do . . ."

(A) *Jake and the Fatman*
(B) *The Golden Girls*
(C) *My Two Dads*
(D) *My Sister Sam*
(E) *You Again?*

GO ON TO THE NEXT PAGE

Crash and Burns

As with one-hit wonders in music,
1980s television had its share of well-known failures.
Here are three of the biggest:

Hector Elizondo
Failure after failure dogged Mr. Elizondo in the 1980s, starting with the ill-fated TV version of *Freebie and the Bean* (1980). Sadly, he played the Bean for only six weeks. Then after a few forgettable roles in movies *(The Fan, Young Doctors in Love)* came forgettable TV roles in *Casablanca* (1983), *a.k.a. Pablo* (1984), *Foley Square* (1986), and the TV version of *Down and Out in Beverly Hills* (1987). He was on track in the '70s (*The Taking of Pelham One Two Three*), and he's a big cheese in the '90s (*Pretty Woman, Chicago Hope*), but the '80s clearly sucked for Hector Elizondo.

Michael Nouri
Sure, he had his *Flashdance,* but Nouri was really nothing more than a flash in the pan. His three quickly cancelled '80s TV series were *The Gangster Chronicles* (1981), *The Bay City Blues* (1983), and *Downtown* (1986). He also starred in *Spraggue,* a 1984 TV pilot about a crime-solving Boston professor that never got made into a series. And you thought Jennifer Beals had bad luck.

Dennis Franz
Typecast early on as a cop, former mailman Franz starred in the short-lived *Chicago Story* (1982), *The Bay City Blues* (1983 — with Michael Nouri!), and *Beverly Hills Buntz* (1987). Sure, he was on the popular *Hill Street Blues* (1985–87), but did you even know Dennis was on it? Were it not for *NYPD Blue* in the '90s, there would be no Dennis Franz.

GO ON TO THE NEXT PAGE

What's my line?

Directions: In this section, you are asked to identify the catchphrase. Each question in this group is made up of a typical scenario from an undisclosed '80s television show, followed by five lettered quotes. Choose the quote that is the most logical response to the scenario.

26. Dudley tells his best friend Arnold Jackson that know-it-all Lisa has the hots for him. What does Arnold say?

    (A) "Dy-no-mite!"
    (B) "I'm gonna get with her."
    (C) "She's an easy lover."
    (D) "What'choo talkin' about, Dudley?"
    (E) "I am the cheese!"

27. Willie Tanner implores his furry houseguest to quit chasing around their cat, Lucky, all the time. The guest employs his stock phrase in response. What is it?

    (A) "I've got dandruff older than you!"
    (B) "No problem!"
    (C) "An alien's gotta eat!"
    (D) "You talkin' to me?"
    (E) "Sit on it, Willie."

28. A plane descends upon a lush island paradise. The white-suited Tattoo sees it, points, and says ——— ?

    (A) "Mr. Roarke, we're under attack!"
    (B) "Here come da fudge!"
    (C) "De plane! De plane!"
    (D) "They're here! They're here!"
    (E) "All aboard!"

29. Sergeant Phil Esterhaus finishes his morning roll call by giving the officers what sage advice before they head off to prowl the streets?

    (A) "Hey, let's be careful out there."
    (B) "Watch your backs."
    (C) "Get your man."
    (D) "Don't eat too many donuts."
    (E) "Make me proud."

30. Murdock's creating havoc for B.A. yet again. After the razzing is over, the gruff, jewelery-encumbered strongman turns to his leader and says what?

    (A) "I don't suffer fools gladly!"
    (B) "Hannibal, make this chump stop."
    (C) "Get this white boy off me!"
    (D) "I pity the fool!"
    (E) "He's on the jazz, man."

31. Chuck Woolery hosted a show where he'd always cut to commercial break the same way. What would he say?

    (A) "Come back and see how this date turned out."
    (B) "Don't turn that dial!"
    (C) "Vanna and I will be waiting for you."
    (D) "Y'all come back now, ya hear?"
    (E) "We'll be back in two minutes, two seconds."

32. Maddie Hayes asks David Addison if he thinks Ms. Dipesto is annoying. How would David assure her that their receptionist is?

    (A) "You bet your sweet bippy."
    (B) "Yes sirree bob!"
    (C) "Si, señorita."
    (D) "Indubitably."
    (E) "Do bees be? Do bears bare?"

GO ON TO THE NEXT PAGE

33. On a Doug Henning special, the long-haired magician makes a leggy blonde disappear. What does he tell the audience?

(A) "Welcome to the world of ill-ooo-sion!"
(B) "She had it coming, the bitch."
(C) "It's just a trick, folks."
(D) "She'll be back."
(E) "Call the police!"

34. Those crafty Duke boys eluded Enos again. What will Rosco P. Coltrane say about this?

(A) "Don't sweat it, Enos."
(B) "Lay off the moonshine, idjit!"
(C) "Enos, you dipstick!"
(D) "Coo coo coo, Enos."
(E) "Go get Cletus over at crazy Cooter's and arrest Uncle Jesse."

35. If someone pissed off Dr. David Banner, what would he say?

(A) "Don't make me angry. You wouldn't like me when I'm angry."
(B) "It's clobberin' time!"
(C) "Bite my green ass!"
(D) "My power is beyond your understanding."
(E) "Don't mess with the bull. You'll get the horns."

The Dukes of Hazzard

GO ON TO THE NEXT PAGE

Shows That Should Have ■arred Robert Urich

Robert Urich has been a television fixture since his *S.W.A.T.* days in the 1970s. He cruised into the '80s in style on *Vega$* (1978–81) and later played a cool Boston detective in *Spenser: For Hire* (1985–88). He also starred in *Gavilan* (1982), which really wasn't any good. But besides his weak foray into movies (*Ice Pirates* et al.), he went largely unemployed for the 1981–82, 1983–84, 1984–85, and 1988–89 seasons. Maybe that's why he had all of those "real bangeroo" headaches. Hindsight casting picks show where he should have gone in those lean years.

1981–82

Father Murphy
Merlin Olsen was beefy and Robert Urich was beefy, but who would you rather watch thwart evil as a member of the cloth? Urich as a clergyman would have been an even better coup than tough guy Robert Blake playing a priest in *Hell Town*.

–OR–

The Dukes of Hazzard
In the spring of 1982, Tom Wopat and John Schneider left the show in a contract disagreement. Instead of picking Robert Urich to fill in as cousin Coy Duke, they went with the forgotten Byron Cherry. A missed opportunity on both sides.

GO ON TO THE NEXT PAGE

Saturday Night Live quote ID

Directions: Below are some memorable quotes from '80s-era *Saturday Night Live* (when it was still good). For each question, you are to look at the quote and select:

(A) if Jon Lovitz said it
(B) if Martin Short said it
(C) if Billy Crystal said it
(D) if Eddie Murphy said it
(E) if Dana Carvey said it

36. "You look mah-velous."

37. "I'm Gumby, dammit."

38. "We're going to pump you up."

39. "My wife's, uh, Morgan Fairchild. Yeah, that's the ticket!"

40. "I get to meet Pat Sajak? I'm so excited, I must say."

41. "Kill my landlord. Kill my landlord. C-I-L-L my landlord."

42. "Worship me. Kneel before me. I am Mephistopheles!"

43. "Look at you, with your bulbous groin region all engorged and tingling."

44. "Can you say 'policeman,' boys and girls?"

45. "Acting!"

46. "You're uns, twis, fee times a mady."

47. "Defensive? I'm not being defensive.
You're the one who's being defensive."

48. "Oooh, I hate it when that happens."

49. "I'm not very strong a swimmer."

50. "I'm chopping broccoli."

1983 – 84

Manimal
Robert Urich morphing into a panther? Meow.

1984 – 85

V.
Urich would have been the perfect foil to the alien race that loved to rip their human faces off. Instead, they gave it to the Beastmaster, Marc Singer. That ain't right.

1988 – 89

Head of the Class
If Howard Hesseman had been canned two years early, like he should have been, Urich could have taught his street smarts to the nerds like Arvid. What better role model is there than the man who hung out with Hawk?

GO ON TO THE NEXT PAGE →

Spinoff City

Directions: The following questions refer to '80s primetime spinoffs. Each question contains a show in capital letters followed by five lettered shows. Choose the show that begat the one in capital letters.

51. *JOANIE LOVES CHACHI*

(A) *Mork & Mindy*
(B) *Laverne & Shirley*
(C) *Fonzie's Funhouse*
(D) *The Happy Days Gang*
(E) *Happy Days*

52. *A DIFFERENT WORLD*

(A) *The Cosby Show*
(B) *Growing Pains*
(C) *Family Ties*
(D) *Fat Albert and the Cosby Kids*
(E) *The Jeffersons*

53. *THE FACTS OF LIFE*

(A) *Silver Spoons*
(B) *It's Tootie!*
(C) *Diff'rent Strokes*
(D) *Taxi*
(E) *Hello, Larry*

54. *A MAN CALLED HAWK*

(A) *Magnum, P.I.*
(B) *Buck Rogers in the 25th Century*
(C) *Spencer*
(D) *Spenser: For Hire*
(E) *Airwolf*

55. *FAMILY MATTERS*

(A) *Full House*
(B) *Perfect Strangers*
(C) *Family Ties*
(D) *Growing Pains*
(E) *It's Urkel!*

56. *BOOKER*

(A) *21 Jump Street*
(B) *T. J. Hooker*
(C) *Jake and the Fatman*
(D) *T. and T.*
(E) *MacGyver*

57. *BEVERLY HILLS BUNTZ*

(A) *Down and Out in Beverly Hills*
(B) *Night Court*
(C) *L.A. Law*
(D) *Hill Street Blues*
(E) *Manimal*

58. *CHECKING IN*

(A) *227*
(B) *The Jeffersons*
(C) *Fat Albert and the Cosby Kids*
(D) *I Love Lucy*
(E) *Making a Living*

GO ON TO THE NEXT PAGE

59. *JUST THE TEN OF US*

    (A) *Gimme a Break*

    (B) *The Brady Bunch*

    (C) *Baker's Dozen*

    (D) *Growing Pains*

    (E) *Three's Company*

60. *LIVING DOLLS*

    (A) *Bosom Buddies*

    (B) *The Wonder Years*

    (C) *Who's the Boss?*

    (D) *Too Close for Comfort*

    (E) *Real People*

The Facts of Life

GO ON TO THE NEXT PAGE

Dallas *vs.* Dynasty
Who Won?

Nighttime soap operas were all the rage in the '80s.
But two, *Dallas* and *Dynasty,* clearly stand ahead of the pack as the best of the genre.
Sure, *Dallas* got better ratings, but as brilliant but little-viewed shows like *It's Your Move* will attest,
ratings aren't what makes a show great.
Which of the two soaps can bill itself as being the best of the '80s?

Category	**Dallas**	**Dynasty**	*Winner*
Setting	Dallas	Denver	*Dallas*
Business	Ewing Oil	Big Oil	*Dallas*
Domicile	Southfork	Carrington mansion	*Dallas*
Blockbuster plotline	"Who Shot J.R.?"	"The Catfight"	*Dallas*
Patriarch	Jock	Blake	*Dynasty*
Matriarch	Miss Ellie	Krystle	*Dynasty*
Brat	Charlene Tilton	Heather Locklear	*Dynasty*
Babe	Victoria Principal	Emma Samms	*Dynasty*
Villian	J.R.	Alexis	pick 'em
Bore	Patrick Duffy	John James	pick 'em
Tiebreaker	Better theme song	Aaron Spelling	*Dallas*

Winner:
Dallas

GO ON TO THE NEXT PAGE

Matching actors to their shows

Directions for questions 61–90: Below are five categories with five questions each. Each question consists of an actor or actress (Column A) and a television show (Column B). In each category, match an actor or actress in Column A to the show in Column B that he or she starred in. (Note: Each show in Column B will be chosen only once per category.)

Bores

A		**B**
61. Kirk Cameron	(A)	*Hunter*
62. Scott Baio	(B)	*Head of the Class*
63. Fred Dryer	(C)	*Diff'rent Strokes*
64. Conrad Bain	(D)	*Growing Pains*
65. Howard Hesseman	(E)	*Charles in Charge*

Boobs

A		**B**
66. Richard Moll	(A)	*Too Close For Comfort*
67. Jm J. Bullock	(B)	*One Day at a Time*
68. Skip Stephenson	(C)	*Night Court*
69. Pat Harrington, Jr.	(D)	*Real People*
70. John Ratzenberger	(E)	*Cheers*

Babes

A		**B**
71. Lisa Bonet	(A)	*The Fall Guy*
72. Catherine Bach	(B)	*A Different World*
73. Teri Copley	(C)	*Too Close for Comfort*
74. Heather Thomas	(D)	*The Dukes of Hazzard*
75. Lydia Cornell	(E)	*We Got It Made*

Hunks

A		**B**
76. Bruce Boxleitner	(A)	*Bring 'Em Back Alive*
77. Stephen Collins	(B)	*Cover Up*
78. Lee Horsley	(C)	*Matt Houston*
79. Richard Dean Anderson	(D)	*Tales of the Gold Monkey*
80. Jon-Erik Hexum	(E)	*MacGyver*

Geeks

A		**B**
81. Dan Frischman	(A)	*Moonlighting*
82. Thom Bray	(B)	*Head of the Class*
83. Curtis Armstrong	(C)	*Family Ties*
84. Josh Saviano	(D)	*The Wonder Years*
85. Marc Price	(E)	*Riptide*

Freaks

A		**B**
86. Christopher Lloyd	(A)	*Misfits of Science*
87. Ron Perlman	(B)	*The Powers of Matthew Star*
88. Peter Barton	(C)	*Beauty and the Beast*
89. Courteney Cox	(D)	*Manimal*
90. Simon MacCorkindale	(E)	*Taxi*

GO ON TO THE NEXT PAGE

Tube analogies

Directions: In each of the following questions, a related pair of names or shows is followed by five lettered pairs of names or shows. Select the lettered pair that best expresses a relationship similar to that expressed in the original pair.

91. Stephanie Zimbalist : Pierce Brosnan ::

    (A) Larry Wilcox : Erik Estrada
    (B) Cybill Shepherd : Bruce Willis
    (C) David Hasselhoff : KITT
    (D) Angela Lansbury : Tom Selleck
    (E) Sharon Gless : Tyne Daly

92. Skippy : Alex P. Keaton ::

    (A) Cooter : Jesse Duke
    (B) Chachi : Richie Cunningham
    (C) Bentley : George Jefferson
    (D) T.C. : Thomas Magnum
    (E) The Gooch : Arnold Jackson

93. Larry : Darryl ::

    (A) Larry : his other brother Larry
    (B) Larry : his other brother Darryl
    (C) Larry : Jack Tripper
    (D) William Sanderson : Peter Scolari
    (E) other brother Darryl : Dick Loudon

94. Mrs. Garrett : Mr. Drummond ::

    (A) Tony Micelli : Angela Bower
    (B) Benson : Governor Gatling
    (C) Small Wonder : Ted Lawson
    (D) Kate Summers : Edward Stratton III
    (E) Webster : George Papadapolis

Diff'rent Strokes

GO ON TO THE NEXT PAGE

95. Bronson Pinchot : Balki Bartokomous ::

(A) Donny Most : Potsie Weber
(B) Lee Horsley : John Houston
(C) Allyce Beasley : Agnes Dipesto
(D) Vic Tayback : Henry Rush
(E) Alfonso Ribeiro : Ricky Stratton

96. Mike Seaver : Boner ::

(A) Arnold Jackson : Willis
(B) Beauty : the Beast
(C) Charles : Willie Aames
(D) Theo Huxtable : Cockroach
(E) Doogie Howser : Wanda

97. John Forsythe : Charlie Townsend ::

(A) Daniel Stern : Kevin Arnold
(B) William Daniels : KITT
(C) Orson Welles : Robin Masters
(D) Mel Blanc : Twiki
(E) all of the above

98. Wink Martindale : Alex Trebec ::

(A) *The New Newlywed Game : Jeopardy!*
(B) *Hollywood Squares : Card Sharks*
(C) *The New Tic Tac Dough : Classic Concentration*
(D) *The New Tic Tac Dough : Pictionary*
(E) *Family Feud : Match Game P.M.*

99. Blake Carrington : Dynasty ::

(A) Gary Ewing : *Knots Landing*
(B) Mr. Roarke : *Fantasy Island*
(C) Jason Colby : *The Colbys*
(D) Jock Ewing : *Dallas*
(E) Captain Stubing : *The Love Boat*

100. Marilyn McCoo : *Solid Gold* ::

(A) Dr. Ruth Westheimer : *Crossfire*
(B) Andy Gibb : *Puttin' on the Hits*
(C) John Davidson : *Real People*
(D) Dick Clark : *Totally Hidden Video*
(E) Adrian Zmed : *Dance Fever*

For the next ten questions, follow the instructions above. In these, however, the first part of the answer pair is given with the original pair. Find the lettered answer that fits the analogy.

101. Howard Hesseman : Arvid :: Hayley Mills :

(A) Screech
(B) The Gooch
(C) Goober
(D) Beans Baxter
(E) Johnny Slash

102. Kermit the Frog : *The Muppet Show* :: Gary Gnu :

(A) *Animals, Animals, Animals*
(B) *Misfits of Science*
(C) *My Little Pony and Friends*
(D) *The Great Space Coaster*
(E) *Pee-wee's Playhouse*

103. Ed McMahon : Johnny Carson :: Doug Llewelyn :

(A) Joseph Wapner
(B) Chuck Woolery
(C) Jim Bakker
(D) David Letterman
(E) Alan Thicke

GO ON TO THE NEXT PAGE

104. St. Eligius : *St. Elsewhere* :: Eastman Medical Center :

(A) *AfterMASH*
(B) *Trapper John, M.D.*
(C) *China Beach*
(D) *Quincy, M.E.*
(E) *Doogie Howser, M.D.*

105. Bob McKenzie : Rick Moranis :: The guy under the seats :

(A) Larry David
(B) Chris Elliott
(C) Dave Foley
(D) Michael Richards
(E) Joe Piscopo

106. Ted Koppel : *ABC News Nightline* :: John Walsh :

(A) *Candid Camera*
(B) *Unsolved Mysteries*
(C) *America's Most Wanted*
(D) *American Gladiators*
(E) *Cops*

107. Greg Evigan : Bear :: Don Johnson :

(A) Gator
(B) Freeway
(C) Melanie Griffith
(D) Bo
(E) Elvis

108. Tom Bosley : *Father Dowling Mysteries* :: Merlin Olsen :

(A) *Tour of Duty*
(B) *Highway to Heaven*
(C) *Father Murphy*
(D) *Webster*
(E) *Hell Town*

109. *She's the Sheriff* : Suzanne Somers :: *Sidekicks* :

(A) Chuck Norris
(B) Brandon Lee
(C) John Ritter
(D) Gil Gerard
(E) Richard Hatch

110. Lt. Worf : Patrick Stewart :: Lt. Howard Hunter :

(A) Daniel J. Travanti
(B) Dennis Franz
(C) Optimus Prime
(D) Richard Dysart
(E) Adam West

GO ON TO THE NEXT PAGE

The Cosby Show *vs.* Family Ties
Who Won?

Bill Cosby was credited with revitalizing the family sitcom at a time
when *Silver Spoons* and *Webster* were the forerunners of the genre.
But *Family Ties* came first and gave us Michael J. Fox.
So which ratings behemoth has bragging rights as the best family sitcom of the decade?
(Note on the tiebreaker: *Leonard Part 6* was Bill Cosby's biggest mistake to date,
and *Light of Day* was a horrible film starring Michael J. Fox and Joan Jett.)

Category	**The Cosby Show**	**Family Ties**	*Winner*
Setting	Brooklyn, New York	Columbus, Ohio	*Cosby Show*
Father	Heathcliff Huxtable	Steven Keaton	*Cosby Show*
Mother	Clair	Elyse	pick 'em
Brother	Theo	Alex P.	*Family Ties*
Hot sister	Lisa Bonet	Justine Bateman	*Cosby Show*
Young sister	Rudy	Jennifer	*Cosby Show*
Other sister	Sabrina Le Beauf	—	*Family Ties*
Other, other sister	Vanessa	—	pick 'em
Boyfriend	Elvin	Nick	*Family Ties*
Family friend	Bud	Skippy	*Family Ties*
Tiebreaker:			
Movie	*Leonard Part 6*	*Light of Day*	*Family Ties*

Winner:
Family Ties!

GO ON TO THE NEXT PAGE

The Cosby Show: story problem

Directions: The passage below describes an unaired episode of *The Cosby Show*. After reading it, answer the four questions that follow.

Cliff and Clair have yet another crisis on their hands when Theo bets his best friend that he can get into a strip club. The Huxtables' only son gets into a mess of trouble when he is arrested for touching one of the strippers. Meanwhile, Rudy flushes Vanessa's favorite earrings down the toilet.

111. The story line, as usual, leaves out the eldest daughter, ———— .

    (A) Vanessa
    (B) Lisa
    (C) Sabrina
    (D) Sondra
    (E) Denise

112. The setting of the earring incident is ———— .

    (A) Brooklyn, New York
    (B) Washington, D.C.
    (C) Chicago, Illinois
    (D) Port Washington, New York
    (E) Philadelphia, Pennsylvania

113. The story doesn't mention the professions of the Huxtable honchos, but ———— .

    (A) Cliff is a surgeon and Clair is a pediatrician
    (B) Cliff is a newspaper reporter and Clair is a nurse
    (C) Cliff owns a junkyard and Clair produces a show called *The Brown Hornet*
    (D) Cliff is an obstetrician and Clair is a legal aid attorney
    (E) Cliff is a pediatrician and Clair is an assistant district attorney

114. Also left out of the story line is the kid who had a crush on Rudy, ———— .

    (A) Cockroach
    (B) Bud
    (C) Jason
    (D) Skippy
    (E) Elvin

115. The character played by Lisa Bonet was not in this episode because she was off at a school named ———— .

    (A) New York University
    (B) Princeton University
    (C) Hillman College
    (D) Lincoln University
    (E) Leland College

116. If this episode had aired, you would have seen it in *The Cosby Show*'s regular time slot on ———— .

    (A) Thursday at 8 p.m.
    (B) Tuesday at 8 p.m.
    (C) Monday at 8 p.m.
    (D) Tuesday at 9 p.m.
    (E) Thursday at 9 p.m.

GO ON TO THE NEXT PAGE

Dallas: a ██tory problem

Directions: The following open letter — apparently never published — was found recently. After reading it, answer questions 117–122.

August 22, 1989

   Dear Emmy voters,

[5] *Our little show, which has been on for eleven seasons already, has never won the coveted Outstanding Drama award. Well, shoot — that's why I took out this Texas-sized ad in all the trades. The show, of course, needs no introduction: it's the same one that* [10] *begat the most popular spin-off of all time, that was also the number one–rated show three times, and had one episode that was the highest rated episode of all time when it aired in 1980. What more do y'all want? We've given you shock, schlock, and Jock. We've* [15] *given you a season that was just a dream. And for Pete's sake, we've given you Charlene Tilton. Now give us our Emmy!*

   Yours sincerely,

   Larry "J. R." Hagman

117. The letter writer focuses mainly on the show called ———— .

   (A) *Knots Landing*
   (B) *Dynasty*
   (C) *General Hospital*
   (D) *Dallas*
   (E) *Falcon Crest*

118. The spin-off mentioned in line 10 is ———— .

   (A) *Falcon Crest*
   (B) *The Colbys*
   (C) *Knots Landing*
   (D) *Flamingo Road*
   (E) *Laverne and Shirley*

119. The high-rated episode in lines 12–13 identified the person who shot J.R. as none other than a character played by ———— .

   (A) Mary Crosby
   (B) Joan Van Ark
   (C) Linda Gray
   (D) Priscilla Presley
   (E) Pamela Sue Martin

120. The dream referred to in line 15 was dreamed by ———— .

   (A) J. R. Ewing
   (B) Hoss Cartwright
   (C) Pamela Ewing
   (D) Bobby Ewing
   (E) Alexis Carrington

121. The actress in line 16 played the role of ———— .

   (A) Miss Ellie, the mother of J.R. and Bobby
   (B) Sue Ellen Ewing, the wife of J.R.
   (C) Lucy Ewing, the daughter of Bobby
   (D) Lucy Ewing, Jock's only daughter
   (E) Lucy Ewing, J.R.'s niece

GO ON TO THE NEXT PAGE

122. Which of the following can be inferred from the letter?

   I.   The letter writer has never won an Emmy.

   II. The letter writer would really like to win the Outstanding Drama Emmy.

   III. The letter writer has the hots for Charlene Tilton.

(A) I only
(B) II only
(C) I and III only
(D) II and III only
(E) All of the above

Dallas

GO ON TO THE NEXT PAGE

Which does not fit?

Directions: Each question below consists of something in capitals, followed by five lettered characters or shows. Choose the lettered character or show that does not fit with the capitalized item.

123. *THE A-TEAM*

  (A) Sgt. "B.A." Baracus
  (B) Capt. Lou Albano
  (C) Capt. "Howlin' Mad" Murdock
  (D) Lt. Templeton Peck
  (E) Col. John Smith

124. *21 JUMP STREET*

  (A) Richard Grieco
  (B) Jason Gedrick
  (C) Peter DeLuise
  (D) Michael DeLuise
  (E) Johnny Depp

125. ORIGINAL *L.A. LAW* CAST MEMBERS

  (A) Michael Tucker
  (B) Blair Underwood
  (C) Jimmy Smits
  (D) Harry Hamlin
  (E) Corbin Bernsen

126. *ST. ELSEWHERE*

  (A) Denzel Washington
  (B) Alfre Woodard
  (C) Mark Harmon
  (D) Grant Goodeve
  (E) Howie Mandel

127. ORIGINAL MTV VJS

  (A) Martha Quinn
  (B) J. J. Jackson
  (C) "Downtown" Julie Brown
  (D) Alan Hunter
  (E) Mark Goodman

128. *SATURDAY NIGHT LIVE*

  (A) Michael Richards
  (B) Anthony Michael Hall
  (C) Joan Cusack
  (D) Robert Downey, Jr.
  (E) Damon Wayans

129. JASON BATEMAN

  (A) *Our House*
  (B) *Little House on the Prairie*
  (C) *Valerie*
  (D) *Silver Spoons*
  (E) *It's Your Move*

130. LATE-NIGHT TALK SHOW HOSTS

  (A) Morton Downey, Jr.
  (B) Pat Sajak
  (C) Dr. Ruth Westheimer
  (D) Arsenio Hall
  (E) Richard Simmons

131. TV CANINES

  (A) Bear
  (B) Boomer
  (C) Freeway
  (D) Ubu
  (E) Brandon

132. SITCOMS ABOUT DIVORCED WOMEN

  (A) *The Days and Nights of Molly Dodd*
  (B) *One Day at a Time*
  (C) *Kate & Allie*
  (D) *Alice*
  (E) *Murphy Brown*

GO ON TO THE NEXT PAGE

133. SITCOMS BASED ON MOVIES

(A) *Fast Times*
(B) *Stir Crazy*
(C) *Gung Ho*
(D) *Nothing in Common*
(E) *Animal House*

134. HUGE MINISERIES

(A) *The Thorn Birds*
(B) *V.*
(C) *The Samurai*
(D) *The Winds of War*
(E) *Shaka Zulu*

135. SHOWS WITH A LIQUOR LICENSE

(A) *Archie Bunker's Place*
(B) *J. J. Starbuck*
(C) *Frank's Place*
(D) *It's a Living*
(E) *Cheers*

136. SHOWS STARRING *TAXI* CAST MEMBERS

(A) *Taxi*
(B) *Wizards and Warriors*
(C) *Dear John*
(D) *Night Court*
(E) *Who's the Boss?*

137. SHOWS SET IN CHICAGO

(A) *Chicago Story*
(B) *Crime Story*
(C) *Joanie Loves Chachi*
(D) *Punky Brewster*
(E) *St. Elsewhere*

Premise descriptions

Directions: A friend of yours remembers the premise of a show but can't recall its name. Can you help him out? Each of the questions below consists of a show's premise followed by five possibilities about its title. Choose the correct lettered show.

138. "It's about this butler who comes to Pittsburgh to run the Owens household and trade barbs with the youngest kid, Wesley."

(A) *Charles in Charge*
(B) *Love, Sidney*
(C) *Benson*
(D) *Who's the Boss?*
(E) *Mr. Belvedere*

139. "Do you remember this one show that took place at a newspaper and starred that guy that was in *Buffalo Bill*? I think it only lasted a year."

(A) *Hooperman*
(B) *The Slap Maxwell Story*
(C) *Anything But Love*
(D) *Perfect Strangers*
(E) *Lou Grant*

140. "It was this Steven Spielberg–produced anthology series that had Kevin Costner in the pilot episode."

(A) *The Twilight Zone*
(B) *Amazing Stories*
(C) *Alfred Hitchcock Presents*
(D) *Wizards and Warriors*
(E) *The Quest*

GO ON TO THE NEXT PAGE

141. "I can't quite remember the name of the show, but it was about this guy named Bogg and a snot-nosed kid, and they would travel through time using a device called the Omni."

(A) *Voyagers!*
(B) *Mr. Merlin*
(C) *Misfits of Science*
(D) *Bring 'Em Back Alive*
(E) *Quantum Leap*

142. "Supposedly this guy was 'one of the family' and he hung out a lot with that kid from *Eight Is Enough*."

(A) *Bosom Buddies*
(B) *Knight Rider*
(C) *Charles in Charge*
(D) *Who's the Boss?*
(E) *Mr. Belvedere*

143. "It was this one reality-based show that had that Messy Marvin kid in it, as well as Byron Allen and some blonde named Sarah something or other."

(A) *Those Amazing Animals*
(B) *Games People Play*
(C) *Real People*
(D) *That's Incredible!*
(E) *Foul-Ups, Bleeps & Blunders*

144. "Did you know that the characters from *The Simpsons* originated on another show that I can't remember the name of?"

(A) *Homer's Family*
(B) *The Tracey Ullman Show*
(C) *It's Garry Shandling's Show*
(D) *Friday Night Videos*
(E) *Fridays*

145. "All I remember about this game show is that people would say, 'No whammies, no whammies!'"

(A) *The Price Is Right*
(B) *Card Sharks*
(C) *The Joker's Wild*
(D) *Press Your Luck*
(E) *Remote Control*

146. "I've only got three words to say about that show: Harlan the mechanic."

(A) *Hill Street Blues*
(B) *Booker*
(C) *G.I. Joe: A Great American Hero*
(D) *CHiPs*
(E) *The Equalizer*

147. "George Clooney and Jason Alexander were in a show that took place in the emergency room of a hospital."

(A) *Trapper John, M.D.*
(B) *The Nurse*
(C) *E/R*
(D) *Trauma Center*
(E) *AfterMASH*

148. "There was this one action show with a character named Cursor and Desi Arnaz, Jr., as a computer expert, and it was really, really bad."

(A) *Knight Rider*
(B) *The Devlin Connection*
(C) *RoboCop*
(D) *Galactica 1980*
(E) *Automan*

Major Stars of the '90s
Who Were on TV
In the '80s

Like George Clooney and Jason Alexander on the show that's the answer for #147, the following '90s stars turned up on network television in the 1980s:

Alec Baldwin, *Knots Landing*

Halle Berry, *Living Dolls*

Jim Carrey, *The Duck Factory*

Courteney Cox, Bruce Springsteen video and *Misfits of Science*

Geena Davis, *Buffalo Bill, Family Ties, Sara*

Johnny Depp, *21 Jump Street*

Andy Garcia, *Hill Street Blues*

Jeff Goldblum, *Tenspeed and Brown Shoe*

Tom Hanks, *Bosom Buddies*

GO ON TO THE NEXT PAGE

149. "The kid in this show had a video game called Swamp Wars."

(A) *Punky Brewster*
(B) *Silver Spoons*
(C) *Diff'rent Strokes*
(D) *Small Wonder*
(E) *Love, Sidney*

150. "After his meal ticket, Apollo Creed, expired in *Rocky IV*, Carl Weathers showed up on some renegade cop show whose name escapes me."

(A) *21 Jump Street*
(B) *Spenser: For Hire*
(C) *Hunter*
(D) *Fortune Dane*
(E) *Sledge Hammer!*

151. "Scott Bakula, later the star of *Quantum Leap*, had the lead role in this series based on a movie."

(A) *Starman*
(B) *Fast Times*
(C) *Stir Crazy*
(D) *Nothing in Common*
(E) *Gung Ho*

152. "A bad-ass helicopter was the real star; pre-*SNL* Dana Carvey, who played Jafo, just rode around in it."

(A) *Airwolf*
(B) *Blue Thunder*
(C) *Riptide*
(D) *Crazy Like a Fox*
(E) *Code Name: Foxfire*

GO ON TO THE NEXT PAGE

153. "All I remember is a paunchy Lee Van Cleef in the title role, Timothy Van Patten as his unbelievable sidekick, and that one of the episodes starred Demi Moore."

   (A) *The Master*
   (B) *Mr. Merlin*
   (C) *The New Adventures of Beans Baxter*
   (D) *Manimal*
   (E) *The White Shadow*

154. "Rob Lowe's less attractive brother, Chad, starred in a great sitcom that died a quick death in the mid-'80s, but that's all I know."

   (A) *It's Your Move*
   (B) *Spencer*
   (C) *Webster*
   (D) *Mr. Merlin*
   (E) *Life Goes On*

155. "It starred Paul Rodriguez and that guy from *The Electric Company*. What a horrible show!"

   (A) *Freebie and the Bean*
   (B) *a.k.a. Pablo*
   (C) *The New Odd Couple*
   (D) *What's Happenin' Now!!*
   (E) *CHiPs*

156. "I remember that someone was always called 'Counseler,' that one of the leads was in *Turk 182!*, and that the main character was originally named Hinkley, but they had to change it to Hanley after Reagan was shot."

   (A) *Jack and Mike*
   (B) *Cover Up*
   (C) *The Greatest American Hero*
   (D) *Hardcastle and McCormick*
   (E) *Today's F.B.I.*

Teri Hatcher, *The Love Boat*

Janet Jackson, *Diff'rent Strokes, Fame*

Demi Moore,
on an episode of *The Master, General Hospital*

Rosie O'Donnell, *Gimme a Break*

Chazz Palminteri, *Hill Street Blues*

Sarah Jessica Parker, *Square Pegs*

Meg Ryan,
One of the Boys, As the World Turns

Jerry Seinfeld, *Benson*

Elisabeth Shue, *Call to Glory*

Madeline Stowe, *The Gangster Chronicles*

Sharon Stone, *The Bay City Blues*

Marisa Tomei, *A Different World*

GO ON TO THE NEXT PAGE

157. "This show showcased Deena Freeman (as hippie niece April), her annoying voice, and her annoying headbands."

    (A) *The Wonder Years*
    (B) *Dynasty*
    (C) *The Golden Girls*
    (D) *Too Close for Comfort*
    (E) *Murder, She Wrote*

158. "Like almost all sitcoms that last too long, they brought in a kid to fulfill the requisite 'cute' factor; the one in this case had red hair and liked to sing country."

    (A) *Diff'rent Strokes*
    (B) *The Cosby Show*
    (C) *Barbara Mandrell & the Mandrell Sisters*
    (D) *Kate & Allie*
    (E) *Family Ties*

159. "There was this goofy show that starred Mr. Stratton from *Silver Spoons* and Meeno Peluce. Like many great sitcoms, it was killed after one season."

    (A) *Private Benjamin*
    (B) *Seven Brides for Seven Brothers*
    (C) *Mr. Smith*
    (D) *Best of the West*
    (E) *Blazing Saddles*

160. " 'Whenever there's trouble, we're there on the double, we're the Bloodhound Gang.' What show was that on, dammit?"

    (A) *The Electric Company*
    (B) *Inspector Gadget*
    (C) *Not Necessarily the News*
    (D) *Sesame Street*
    (E) *3–2–1 Contact*

161. "When Ted McGinley was brought in as nephew Roger Phillips, you knew this show was about to go under."

    (A) *Happy Days*
    (B) *Married . . . with Children*
    (C) *Dynasty*
    (D) *Hart to Hart*
    (E) *The Love Boat*

162. "Two of its characters were Danny Amatullo and Leroy Johnson."

    (A) *Diff'rent Strokes*
    (B) *Fame*
    (C) *A New Kind of Family*
    (D) *Paper Dolls*
    (E) *The Facts of Life*

GO ON TO THE NEXT PAGE

Dumb Cartoon Characters
of the 1980s

Scrappy-Doo: he ruined Scooby

Godzooky: Like Gleek before him, the younger Godzilla was there strictly for laughs. Except he wasn't funny, so why was he there?

The Shmoo: What the hell was that thing? A marshmallow? A wad of goo? No, the Shmoo!

Snarf from *ThunderCats:* Snarf, snarf, I'm stupid, snarf.

Orko from *He-Man and the Masters of the Universe*: Completely unbelievable magician sidekick for the guy who repelled Skeletor's evil horde with ease.

Teddy Ruxpin: Don't get me started.

Any of the Smurfs (particularly Brainy): La, la, la-la, la, la, sing a happy song! Smurf you!

The Littles: These munchkins were only slightly less annoying than . . .

The Monchhichis

GO ON TO THE NEXT PAGE

Daytime TV

Directions: The following questions test your knowledge of daytime television. Each question contains an incomplete sentence followed by five lettered answers. Choose the one that best completes the sentence.

163. *General Hospital's* Luke was played by Anthony Geary, while Laura was played by ———— .

   (A) Pamela Sue Martin
   (B) Genie Francis
   (C) Finola Hughes
   (D) Mare Winningham
   (E) Emma Samms

164. Susan Lucci never won an Emmy for her portrayal of ———— .

   (A) Erica
   (B) Cloey
   (C) Deidre
   (D) Shannon
   (E) Victoria

165. All of the following had '80s daytime talk shows EXCEPT ———— .

   (A) Regis Philbin
   (B) Geraldo Rivera
   (C) Richard Simmons
   (D) Sally Jessy Raphäel
   (E) Oprah Winfrey

166. Jack Wagner, who sang "All I Need," was on ———— .

   (A) *Santa Barbara*
   (B) *General Hospital*
   (C) *One Life to Live*
   (D) *The Young and the Restless*
   (E) *The Bold and the Beautiful*

167. Michael Damian, who sang "Rock On," was on ———— .

   (A) *The Bold and the Beautiful*
   (B) *General Hospital*
   (C) *Guiding Light*
   (D) *Days of Our Lives*
   (E) *The Young and the Restless*

168. Gloria Loring, who sang "Friends and Lovers," was on ———— .

   (A) *General Hospital*
   (B) *Days of Our Lives*
   (C) *Another World*
   (D) *Santa Barbara*
   (E) *The Guiding Light*

169. On *General Hospital,* Rick Springfield played a ———— .

   (A) lawyer
   (B) homeless man
   (C) reporter
   (D) musician
   (E) doctor

170. Bob McGrath could regularly be seen on ———— .

   (A) *The Great Space Coaster*
   (B) *Captain Kangaroo*
   (C) *Sesame Street*
   (D) *Days of Our Lives*
   (E) *Mister Rogers' Neighborhood*

GO ON TO THE NEXT PAGE

171. The daytime talk show host who dressed in drag for one show was ——— .

(A) Richard Simmons
(B) Phil Donahue
(C) Regis Philbin
(D) Oprah Winfrey
(E) Geraldo Rivera

172. The daytime talk show host who got punched on the air was ——— .

(A) Richard Simmons
(B) Morton Downey, Jr.
(C) Phil Donahue
(D) Geraldo Rivera
(E) Sally Jessy Raphäel

173. Scorpio could be found regularly on ——— .

(A) *Loving*
(B) *Santa Barbara*
(C) *General Hospital*
(D) CBS
(E) NBC

174. All of the following had a regular role on *General Hospital* EXCEPT ——— .

(A) Elizabeth Taylor
(B) Richard Simmons
(C) Demi Moore
(D) Shaun Cassidy
(E) Wesley Snipes

175. The woman who played Marlena on *Days of Our Lives* also starred in ——— .

(A) *Cats* on Broadway
(B) *Our House*
(C) *Life Goes On*
(D) *All My Children*
(E) *Santa Barbara*

176. Jim Carrey's ex-wife, Lauren Holly, was a regular cast member of ——— .

(A) *As the World Turns*
(B) *The Young and the Restless*
(C) *All My Children*
(D) *General Hospital*
(E) *Days of Our Lives*

177. None of the following Brat Packers starred in an *ABC Afterschool Special* EXCEPT ——— .

(A) Anthony Michael Hall
(B) Rob Lowe
(C) Molly Ringwald
(D) Ally Sheedy
(E) Judd Nelson

GO ON TO THE NEXT PAGE

Quick and Painful

Five shows that died too soon:

Buck Rogers in the 25th Century
(1979–81) From the lovable robot Twiki ("Beedy-beedy-beedy") to the "Mighty nice shootin', Colonel" Gary Coleman episode, Buck Rogers was a can't-miss show every week, if for nothing else than Erin Gray's hot suits.

Voyagers!
(1982–83) Starring the ill-fated Jon-Erik Hexum and Punky Brewster's brother, Meeno Peluce, this show about a time-traveling tandem was both entertaining and educational. With the help of a cool gizmo, the duo would meet three or four historical figures every week (such as Thomas Edison) and then, like *Quantum Leap* after it, fix mistakes in the timeline. If it had lasted longer, Hexum, who accidently shot himself on the set of *Cover Up* in 1984, might well be alive today.

Max Headroom
(1987) While you probably remember this show as being huge (and earlier in the decade), it actually tanked after only a few episodes. But Max, a stuttering computerized star of futuristic television, spoke more of '80s consumerism than any "Where's the Beef?" ad ever could. Max Headroom's legacy is in the Ronald Reagan *Doonesbury* parody, the Art of Noise song "Paranoimia," and the slew of New Coke commercials promoting the slogan "Catch the Wave."

Fill in the blanks

Directions: Each sentence below has one or two blanks, each blank indicating that something has been omitted. Beneath the sentence are five lettered names or shows or sets of names or shows. Choose the answer for each blank that best fits the meaning of the sentence as a whole.

Questions 178–183 refer to annoying Saturday-morning TV characters.

Unfortunately, Saturday morning TV had its heyday in the '60s and '70s. Maybe that's why there was a slew of truly disturbing Saturday morning characters in the '80s.

178. Even though the tiny creatures called the ——— only had one female in their annoying patriarchal clan, a baby somehow turned up; it was never explained how.

(A) Snorks
(B) Wuzzles
(C) Monchhichis
(D) Smurfs
(E) Littles

179. ——— was an ugly amorphous blob that looked like a cross between Casper the Friendly Ghost and Ronald McDonald's pal Grimace, while the diminuitive ——— loved a mystery and used to say, "Lemme at 'im, lemme at 'im."

(A) Ziggy; Orko
(B) The Shmoo; Scrappy-Doo
(C) Nell Carter; Emmanuel Lewis
(D) Teddy Ruxpin; Captain Caveman
(E) Slimer; Baby-Pac

180. Jonny Quest's bulldog, ———— , barked so much that you wanted to kick it, while his friend ———— wore a turban and was pretty much dead weight.

    (A) Gordon; Galacticus
    (B) Bandit; Hadji
    (C) Meatball; Apu
    (D) Ralph; Hakeem
    (E) Tiger; Race

181. The really disturbing trend of updating old shows by making younger versions of established characters started with ———— .

    (A) *Muppet Babies*
    (B) *The Adventures of Raggedy Ann and Andy*
    (C) *A Pup Named Scooby-Doo*
    (D) *The Flintstone Kids*
    (E) *The Gary Coleman Show*

182. The greatest earthquake ever known plunged Marshall, Will and Holly down 1,000 feet to a land inhabited by the Sleestack and proto-human inhabitants such as ———— .

    (A) Foofur
    (B) Kissyfur
    (C) Chaka
    (D) Ooklah
    (E) Cheetarah

183. The sole purpose of ———— was to be cute, yet its noises and antics were so maddening that it threatened to undermine the coolness of ———— .

    (A) Godzooky; *The Godzilla Show*
    (B) Uni; *Dungeons & Dragons*
    (C) Snarf; *ThunderCats*
    (D) Gleek the Space Monkey; *Super Friends*
    (E) All of the above

Square Pegs

(1982–83) Besides having the great theme song by the Waitresses, *Square Pegs* featured then unknowns Jami Gertz as Muffy, the "Pat Benatar without the chipmunk cheeks;" Sarah Jessica Parker as desperately-seeking-popularity Patty; and Tracy Nelson as Valley Girl Jennifer DeNuccio. That's not even counting New Wave music lover Johnny Slash (Merritt Butrick) and video-game freak Marshall Blechtman (John Femia). God, I miss that show.

It's Your Move

(1984–85) One of the funniest shows of all time, *It's Your Move* starred Jason Bateman as a little schemer who tried to get the goat of his mom's equally scheming boyfriend, Norman Lamb (David Garrison). His fat best friend Eli was often the butt of many cruel jokes and was referred to as "The Wall" in the memorable soccer episode when he played a goalie. If you remember what the Dregs of Humanity were, you probably wish you'd had a VCR back then.

GO ON TO THE NEXT PAGE

Questions 184–192 refer to
Aaron Spelling shows.

In the '80s there were television producers and then there was Aaron Spelling. The following shows refer to his brilliant and not-so-brilliant progeny (no, not Tori).

184. Gopher was the yeoman-purser on *The Love Boat*, Adam Bricker was the ship's wolfish doctor, and ———— was the friendly bartender.

   (A) Freddie "Boom Boom" Washington
   (B) Julie McCoy
   (C) Isaac Washington
   (D) Merill Stubing
   (E) Isaac Hayes

185. The dog's name on ———— was Freeway.

   (A) *Hart to Hart*
   (B) *Fantasy Island*
   (C) *Here's Boomer*
   (D) *Hotel*
   (E) *Vega$*

186. The only Angel who was on the entire run of *Charlie's Angels* was the fetching ———— .

   (A) Kate Smith
   (B) Kate Jackson
   (C) Cheryl Ladd
   (D) Shelley Hack
   (E) Jaclyn Smith

The Love Boat

GO ON TO THE NEXT PAGE

187. The woman who played bitchy Princess Ardala on *Buck Rogers in the 25th Century* was the sexy costar of ——— .

(A) *T. J. Hooker*
(B) *Matt Houston*
(C) *Sidekicks*
(D) *MacGruder and Loud*
(E) *Heartbeat*

188. While her more memorable gig was playing the greedy Sammy Jo on *Dynasty*, ——— simultaneously played Officer Stacy Sheridan on ——— .

(A) Pamela Sue Martin; *Hardcastle and McCormick*
(B) Emma Samms; *The Colbys*
(C) Catherine Oxenberg; *Manimal*
(D) Heather Locklear; *T. J. Hooker*
(E) Heather Thomas; *The Fall Guy*

189. The two catfights between Krystle and ——— were things of TV legend; Krystle's affair with a character played by HIV-positive ——— was a thing of TV tabloids.

(A) Alexia; Cary Grant
(B) Alexis; Rock Hudson
(C) Alex; Rock Hudson
(D) Alexis; Paul Newman
(E) Alexis; Liberace

190. Ricardo Montalban, who had a small Tattoo on ——— , also played the evil Zach Powers on ——— .

(A) *Fantasy Island; The Colbys*
(B) *Fantasy Island; Fantasy Island*
(C) *The Love Boat; Fantasy Island*
(D) *Fantasy Island; Hotel*
(E) *Fantasy Island; The Powers of Matthew Star*

191. William Shatner schooled hunky ——— on *T. J. Hooker;* ——— played the handsome Jeff Colby on both *Dynasty* and *The Colbys*.

(A) George Clooney; Scott Baio
(B) John Stamos; John James
(C) Dweezil Zappa; Rick Springfield
(D) Willie Aames; Grant Goodeve
(E) Adrian Zmed; John James

192. The legendary Bette Davis, who was supposed to be a cast member, appeared in only the pilot of ——— , while the legendary ——— played Dan Tanna's boss in *Vega$*.

(A) *The Colbys;* Gregory Peck
(B) *Dynasty;* James Mason
(C) *Hotel;* Tony Curtis
(D) *T. J. Hooker;* Sidney Poitier
(E) *Matt Houston;* Lucille Ball

GO ON TO THE NEXT PAGE

TV commercials.

Television advertising has been around since the beginning of time (or at least since the invention of the boob tube), but it wasn't until the capitalism-fueled '80s that it began to get truly creative. Evidence follows.

193. Spike Lee's character in the Air Jordan Nike commercials was ——— .

   (A) Mars Blackmon
   (B) Charles Rocket
   (C) River Jordan
   (D) Venus Flytrap
   (E) Fred "The Dorf" Dorfman

194. A commercial for a music compilation called ——— had a hippie saying, "Well, turn it up, dude!"

   (A) *Super Sounds of the '70s*
   (B) *Freedom Rock*
   (C) *Still the '60s*
   (D) *Rock 'n' Roll Rampage*
   (E) *American Pie*

195. Probably the most memorable advertisements for ——— starred ——— , who said, "You have my word on it!"

   (A) Coca-Cola; Mean Joe Greene
   (B) Domino's Pizza; the Noid
   (C) Pepsi; Michael Jackson
   (D) Isuzu; Joe Isuzu
   (E) Coca-Cola; Lyle Alzado

196. Jim Varney's character, ——— , appeared in milk commercials saying, "Hey, Vern"; while ——— told us that Quaker Oats were "the right thing to do."

   (A) "Crocodile" Dundee; King Vitamin
   (B) Ernest; Andy Griffith
   (C) Barney; Howard Hesseman
   (D) Elmo; Dr. Ruth Westheimer
   (E) Ernest; Wilford Brimley

197. Before the tough ——— started going and going and going, Eveready's memorable ads starred tough guy ——— , who double-dared people to knock a battery off his shoulder.

   (A) Snuggles; Mr. T
   (B) Energizer Bunny; Robert Conrad
   (C) Pillsbury Doughboy; Jan Michael Vincent
   (D) Energizer Bunny; Robert Urich
   (E) Jolly Green Giant; Chuck Norris

198. The tiny ——— were so popular they got their own cartoon in 1989; Clara Peller, even more famous for saying ——— , had a role in the 1985 flick *Moving Violations*.

   (A) M&M's candies; "I've fallen and I can't get up!"
   (B) Emmanuel Lewis and Gary Coleman; "It's a meatball!"
   (C) Drano scrub brushes; "Parts is parts"
   (D) California Raisins; "Where's the beef?"
   (E) Smurfs; "That's not a sausage!"

GO ON TO THE NEXT PAGE

199. ——— hawked Chrysler Cordobas with rich Corinthian leather, while Billy Dee Williams was on the case for ——— .

(A) Bruce Willis; Seagram's wine coolers
(B) Herve Villechaise; Velveeta cheese
(C) Ricardo Montalban; Colt .45 malt liquor
(D) John Forsythe; Colt .45 malt liquor
(E) Emma Samms; Coors beer

200. Peter Billingsley, who played the lead role in the 1983 film *A Christmas Story*, also poured ——— as the adorable ——— .

(A) Budweiser; Spuds MacKenzie
(B) frozen juice on a toothpick; Time for Timer
(C) Nestlé Quik; Messy Marvin
(D) Yoplait; Mr. Goodbody
(E) Hershey's Chocolate Syrup; Messy Marvin

STOP*!*

You have reached the end of Section IV

In the interest of space, I have included an explanation of the answer only if there might be some confusion, if a few words should be said on the subject, or if there's a good joke in it. But if you're, like, still confused, you can e-mail me at ***jhaggis@ix.netcom.com.*** (To figure your PCAT result, see, "How to Figure Out Your Score.")

Section I — *The Rad '80s*

Timeline matching
(20 questions)

1. B
2. A
3. E
4. C
5. D
6. C
7. B
8. E
9. A
10. D
11. D
12. A
13. C
14. B
15. E
16. A
17. D
18. E
19. B
20. C

'80s slang
(8 questions)

21. **C.** "Dweeb" and "geek" are almost interchangeable. They both have various derogatory meanings; if somebody calls you either one, it pretty much means you're a loser.

22. **C.** "Gnarly" means "out of sight" or "groovy." You can eliminate (A) "Psych!" which means "Gotcha!"; (B) "Grody to the max" because that means "really gross"; (D), which is self-explanatory; and (E), which means "I hear that" or "You said it." (C) "Totally tubular!" is the most similar, folks.

23. **A.** To take a chill pill would be to relax. Spazzes can't relax. Compare.

24. **D.** "Bodacious" is Valspeak for "awesome" or "outrageous," as in "That chick has bodacious ta-tas." (D) is most correct because a "studmuffin" is almost necessarily bodacious. A "flamer," in (A), is an openly gay male, or a guy who might appear to be

such. (B) "Bogue" means "gross," as does (C) "barf-o-rama." (E) "Butt ugly" speaks for itself.

25. **E.** "Take off, hoser" is the Canadian way of saying "fuck off." A "hoser" is a jerk. Bob and Doug McKenzie (Rick Moranis and Dave Thomas) used this phrase often on SCTV and in the movie *Strange Brew,* as well as in the song "Take Off to the Great White North."

26. **D.** If your car is "bitchin'," it's cool, awesome, or "wicked." Camaros were the most bitchin' cars of the 1980s. (By the way, "hellacious," in (A), means "exceedingly difficult.")

27. **B.** "Gag me with a spoon!" is Valspeak for "disgusting" or "majorly gross." A guy who's "queer" (C), isn't gay, just weird.

28. **E.** "Smooth move, Ex-Lax" was a sarcastic term based on a laxative effect that meant you screwed up, or did something "lame."

Fashion fill in the blanks
(10 questions)

29. **A**
30. **D**
31. **C**
32. **E**
33. **D**
34. **C**
35. **A**
36. **B**
37. **A**
38. **E**

Video games fill in the blanks
(5 questions)

39. **C**
40. **B**
41. **C**
42. **A**
43. **D**

Video games logic

(2 questions)

44. **D.** *Wokka-wokka-wokka-wokka.* The pursuit of the blinking blue ghosts after eating a power pellet is one of the most teeth-clenching parts of Pac-Man. Will your guy get there before Inky reverts to his normal color? If you manage to gobble up all four, you'll have a 3,000-point meal—200 for the first ghost, 400 for the second, 800 for the third, and 1,600 for the last.

45. **C.** Although it may seem like this problem has many possible answers, four universally accepted arcade rules will help you to figure it out: 1) you will spend as many tokens as you can, 2) nothing (not even Frogger) is worth being grounded for a week, 3) no video gamer would watch Skee-Ball (a boring bowling game) with a pocketful of tokens, and 4) if a Frogger master were hogging the game you would either put a token on the game to claim "next" or spend your tokens on other games (like Mappy or Star Wars). These very important arcade guidelines, and the most basic of math skills, negate answers (A), (B), (D) and (E). You'll leave Chuck E. Cheese with three tokens, which you'll spend on your next visit tomorrow.

Which doesn't fit?

(10 questions)

46. **D.** The Hustle was a disco step, which thankfully died as the '80s began.

47. **E.** Red could have been a new category, The Rad '80s!

48. **A.** Black was a color only if you got stuck and peeled off a sticker.

49. **A.** But the only really good Rubik's product was the cube.

50. **D.** Moe was like the fifth Beatle.

51. **B.** Mister Mouth was that great game where you had to flip chips into a spinning yellow head.

52. **E.** It was the Atari 2400, a higher step in the video-game food chain. But nothing could touch IntelliVision.

53. **C.** Zork was an impossibly cool text-only adventure game for the computer.

54. **E.** There was nothing worse than a D&D player who insisted on being a paladin.

55. **A.** Video games began in the '70s with Pong, Asteroids, and Space Invaders but didn't really become cool until Pac-Man hit the arcades in 1980.

'80s analogies
(7 questions)

Names in the news

56. C. Magic was coached by slick-haired Riley on the Lakers, just like 300-pounds-plus Refrigerator Perry was by Da Bears' slick-haired Ditka.

57. E. Smiling gymnast Retton was seemingly on every box of Wheaties after the '84 Olympics, and Senator O'Neill pitched more than politics in Hush Puppies shoes ads.

58. C. Beauty Brinkley married beast Joel, just like model-babe Porizkova wedded Cars' bobo Ocasek.

59. C. Though their subjects were very different, Cosby's *Fatherhood* and Collins's *Hollywood Wives* were both '80s best-sellers.

60. E. Belushi's 1982 OD made huge headlines two years before Marvin Gaye's death. (His father shot him.)

61. A. Bakker's embezzlement was just one of his many crimes to humanity. Von Bülow's offense was portrayed by Jeremy Irons in the movie *Reversal of Fortune*.

62. D. The dastardly duo Penn and Madonna both wed and divorced in the '80s. Of the five choices, only Sly and Nielsen shared the same fate.

'80s phenomena ID
(8 questions)

63. A
64. C
65. D
66. E
67. C
68. B
69. B
70. D

Reagan story problem
(10 questions)

71. E
72. C
73. D
74. A
75. E
76. D
77. D
78. B
79. D
80. C

Section II — *Flicks*

Brat Pack logic
(4 questions)

1. **D.** The seminal Molly Ringwald film *Pretty in Pink* also starred Andrew McCarthy as a "richie," so you know by the third rule that they're the only Brat Packers in it. Un-Brat Jon Cryer is thrown in because he was and always will be "the Duckman."

2. **A.** Since Ally Sheedy was in *The Breakfast Club,* you know by the first rule that Emilio Estevez must be in it, too. And, yes, Judd Nelson (C), who played burnout John Bender, always had a dumb look on his face, especially when he said, "Fix me turkey pot pie."

3. **B.** Unfortunately, Anthony Michael Hall and Ringwald were snubbed in favor of Rob Lowe and Mare Winningham. Just watch *Sixteen Candles* to see how well the two absentees worked together (e.g., "Can I borrow your underpants for five minutes?").

4. **C.** The only two Brat Packers never to work together, Demi Moore and Anthony Michael Hall, appeared in only one of the three films each. Note: Hall turned down Jon Cryer's *Pretty in Pink* role because he didn't want to be typecast as a geek. It didn't work.

Brat Pack multiple choice
(6 questions)

5. **C**
6. **E**
7. **E**
8. **A**
9. **B**
10. **D**

Saturday Night Live alumni matching
(15 questions)

11. **E**
12. **D**
13. **C**
14. **E**
15. **E**
16. **A**
17. **E**
18. **C**
19. **B**
20. **C**
21. **A**
22. **C**
23. **E**
24. **C**
25. **E**

SNL:
The Next Generation matching
(10 questions)

26. B
27. A
28. B
29. B
30. E
31. A
32. D
33. E
34. D
35. C

Location analogies
(5 questions)

36. **D.** Jennifer Beals was a flashdancing steel-worker in Pittsburgh.

37. **A.** *A Room with a View* took place in Florence, *Wall Street* and *Arthur* were set in New York, and *My Left Foot* was in Dublin.

38. **C.** Quick: Where does *Doctor Detroit* take place?

39. **B.** I *Suspect* that Dennis Quaid and Cher got on famously in the nation's capital.

40. **E.** The former home of baseball's Cleveland Indians, Municipal Stadium, used to be called the "Mistake by the Lake." The same could be said of *Howard the Duck*.

Memorable roles analogies
(20 questions)

41. **D.** In the detective spoof *Who's Harry Crumb? Who cares?*

42. A

43. **C.** *Ferris Bueller's Day Off* quote: "When Cameron was in Egypt land, let my Cameron go-o-o."

44. E
45. C

46. **D.** "Tell 'em Large Marge sent ya."

47. **C.** "What's a-happenin', hot stuff?"

48. A

49. **D.** How much O'Keeffe is in *Tarzan, the Ape Man*? Miles O'Keeffe.

50. A
51. E
52. C
53. D

54. **A.** In *Bull Durham*.

55. **A.** Lobot was Lando Calrissian's cool, bald sidekick in Cloud City.

56. **B.** From *Lethal Weapon 2* and *3*: "Whatever Leo wants, Leo Getz. Get it? Okay, okay, okay."

57. **C.** Argyle was Bruce Willis's nosy limo driver who listened to Run-D.M.C.'s "Christmas in Hollis."

58. B
59. C
60. E

Name the film

(20 questions)

61. C

62. **B.** Future Valley guy Nicolas Cage was billed under his given name, Nicholas Coppola.

63. E
64. D
65. D
66. E
67. C

68. **D.** Costner played the corpse, using more facial expression than usual.

69. A
70. E
71. E
72. C
73. B
74. B
75. D
76. A
77. D
78. C
79. A
80. B

Name the actor

(20 questions)

81. D
82. C
83. B

84. **C.** *Road House* quote: "It's my way or the highway."

85. B
86. E
87. D
88. A
89. D
90. C

91. **C.** Of the two Coreys, it was Feldman, not Haim, that starred in *The Goonies*.

92. E
93. E
94. B
95. D
96. B
97. A

98. **E.** But what hasn't James Earl Jones been in?

99. E
100. C

A few Guttenberg questions
(7 questions)

101. B
102. E
103. C
104. D
105. A

106. C. Although a little kid who was rumored to have hanged himself was supposedly behind a curtain in one scene of this film (*Three Men and a Baby*), it was just a cardboard cutout of the struggling actor played by Ted Danson.

107. B

Matthew Broderick logic
(8 questions)

108. C

109. E. Joshua's creator, Professor Falken, gave his computer the name of his dead son.

110. B. Joshua challenged Broderick to chess; Broderick also played Joshua in tic-tac-toe.

111. A
112. D
113. B
114. E

115. D. He wasn't an IRA terrorist or anything. Broderick was acquitted of vehicular manslaughter after he got in a car accident while driving in Northern Ireland with then-girlfriend Jennifer Grey (his sister in *Ferris Bueller's Day Off*).

Action movie quote ID
(10 questions)

116. D
117. C
118. E
119. B
120. E
121. D
122. A
123. E
124. E
125. C

Comedy movie quote ID

(20 questions)

126. B. Bill Murray, covered in ectoplasm.

127. C. Michael J. Fox, trying to score some alcohol.

128. C. Judge Smails (Ted Knight), admonishing his idiot nephew, Spaulding.

129. C. John Candy, at the big Blues Brothers concert.

130. E. Bruno Kirby, taking a wild stab at a bad Pictionary drawing.

131. B. Chevy Chase, reponding to a shady offer by Tim Matheson.

132. D. Tortured teen Molly Ringwald, after giving her knickers to Anthony Michael Hall.

133. C. Nicolas Cage, before robbing a convenience store.

134. C. Eddie Murphy, passing out snacks.

135. E. Francis had just said, "If anyone touches any of my stuff, I'll kill him."

136. A. Paul Hogan, comparing knives.

137. C. Robert De Niro, very annoyed with Charles Grodin on a bus.

138. A. A geek, in reference to a dance step that Patrick Dempsey was attempting. Another great *Can't Buy Me Love* quote: "You shit on my house, man. You shit on my house."

139. D. Jamie Lee Curtis, to Kevin Kline.

140. A. Michael Caine, to Ruprecht the Monkey Boy (Steve Martin).

141. B. The little kid, unsuccessfully trying to save his folks from a toaster.

142. B. Howard the Duck. But everyone laughed at the movie.

143. A. John Lithgow's imperious alien, showing his disdain for humans.

144. D. John Candy, to a mean principal.

145. C. The brother of Tom Hanks's character, lamenting about hookers not showing up for the bachelor party.

John Hughes

(10 questions)

146. **E.** Mr. Rooney, of Ferris's school record.

147. **B.** Tormented teen Jon Cryer, referring to Andrew McCarthy's oddly named character.

148. **D.** When the Griswolds get lost in St. Louis, they get ridiculed for their ugly car, the Family Truckster.

149. **C.** Judd Nelson, asking the geek (Anthony Michael Hall) for his "doobage."

150. **A.** Though Culkin was in *Rocket Gibraltar* the year before *Uncle Buck,* nobody saw that.

151. **B.** Steve Martin's character, after he slept with John Candy's.

152. **D.** The Griswolds, again, where they won the fateful trip to Europe.

153. **B.** The Geek (Anthony Michael Hall), in the following exchange: "Can I ask you a question?" Samantha (Molly Ringwald): "Yes, you are a total fag." The Geek: "That's not the question."

154. **E.** What someone asks after Anthony Michael Hall's geeky character says he got kicked in the groin.

155. **D.** Mary Stuart Masterson's tomboy, to Eric Stoltz on the big date with Amanda Jones (Lea Thompson).

Steven Spielberg

(10 questions)

156. **D**

157. **B.** Another great quote: "He chose poorly."

158. **E.** E.T. boozed up on Coors, and Henry Thomas felt the effects and set free the frogs in biology class.

159. **B.** The mogwai are the cute pre-Gremlin things. Executive-produced by Spielberg.

160. **D.** Irving provided the singing voice for Jessica Rabbit. Spielberg produced the movie.

161. **C**

162. **E.** Feldman was also in *Gremlins* without Haim. From a story by Spielberg.

163. **E.** Spielberg's *The Color Purple* was also nominated for best picture.

164. **A**

165. **A.** Indiana Jones's miniature sidekick, Short Round.

Spielberg, Part II
(5 questions)

166. **E.** Made $400 million

167. **A.** $242 million

168. **D.** $197 million

169. **C.** $180 million

170. **B.** $148 million

Oscar picks
(10 questions)

171. **D**
172. **C**
173. **A**
174. **E**
175. **A**
176. **C**
177. **D**
178. **B**
179. **E**
180. **C**

Movie musicians fill in the blanks
(10 questions)

181. **C.** Seriously. If you missed the question, put down your pencil and shut the book. I mean it.

182. **E.** This movie came before "If I Could Turn Back Time."

183. **B.** John Lurie of the Lounge Lizards, that is.

184. **B.** Michael J. Fox and Joan Jett — not a good match.

185. **A.** Opposite Blair Underwood (*L.A. Law*) and a whole host of old-school rappers.

186. **D.** That was after she married Spicoli (Sean Penn).

187. **D.** Both were very, very bad movies.

188. **E.** *Nomads* was a thriller starring Pierce Brosnan and "Goody Two Shoes" Ant.

189. **C.** Sting sported red hair in this one.

190. **D.** Bowie's a talented actor; Wiedlin is not.

Teenagers in lust fill in the blanks
(10 questions)

191. B. Peter Billingsley was Messy Marvin, not a studmuffin.

192. C

193. C. "Yo, Mallory!"

194. B
195. D
196. E

197. A. And they were, too.

198. E
199. E
200. B

Section III — *Tunes*

Music math
(8 questions)

1. C. The Thompson Twins numbered three, so $3 \times 6 \div 2 - 3 = 6$

2. D. There were three Banana babes and six INXSers.

3. D. 5150 - 1984 = 3166. And Van Halen minus Diamond Dave equals crap.

4. A. 867-5309. Add it up.

5. D. x = 99.

6. E. Timbuk 3 times nuh-nuh-nuh-nuh-19.

7. B. The difference between Prince's *1999* and Eurythmics' *1984* is the same as that between *1984* and Bryan Adams's "Summer of [19]69."

8. C. Haircut 100's equation was "Love Plus One." Nikki Sixx was the Crüe's bassist. Put the two together and you've got seven times the mess.

Name the musical guru

(12 questions)

9. **D.** Dee Snider & Co. didn't need no stinkin' musical gurus. They spit on musical gurus!

10. **A.** But that's pretty easy, no?

11. **C.** The musical gurus didn't get along. Only MJ was in on this big one.

12. **D.** Nobody had to help the DeBarge family singers.

13. **A.** The artist formerly known as Morris Day.

14. **B.** Rick James later went to the Big House.

15. **A.** Prince wrote it under the pseudonym Christopher. That guy's got more names than Sybil.

16. **A.** Prince first recorded it; Chaka made it famous.

17. **C.** One-hit wonder had his one hit because Jacko was watching him.

18. **A.** Man, Sheena Easton was hot.

19. **B.** Not as good as Eddie's *48 HRS.* cover of "Roxanne."

20. **D.** Stewart took his clothes off alone, thankfully.

Lyric ID

(42 questions)

21. **B**
22. **E**
23. **C**
24. **C.** "He just smiled and gave me a Vegamite sandwich."

25. **A**
26. **E**
27. **A**
28. **E**
29. **D**
30. **B**
31. **B**
32. **B**
33. **E**
34. **A**
35. **C**
36. **E**
37. **C**
38. **C**
39. **A**
40. **E**
41. **E**
42. **B**
43. **A**
44. **D**
45. **C**
46. **D**
47. **B**
48. **D**
49. **C**
50. **D**
51. **C**
52. **B**
53. **C**
54. **C**
55. **E**
56. **D**

57. D
58. B
59. C
60. D
61. D
62. D

Duran Duran story problem

(6 questions)

63. **E.** But that's silly.

64. **B.** This is serious business.

65. **D.** The band member with the biggest solo hit (E) was John Taylor, the bassist, who landed at #23 with "I Do What I Do . . . " from the *9½ Weeks* soundtrack.

66. **C.** It was a pretty lame video, but a great song.

67. **A.** Roger, Nick, and the singer, Simon Le Bon, produced one album, *So Red the Rose.*

68. **E.** You know that (I) is correct, although none of the Taylors were related; (III) also follows from the passage, but most guys wore too much makeup in the '80s. While the passage implies that Roger didn't get much mail in relation to the other fellows, it doesn't mention how much mail (or little girls' panties, for that matter) he or the other boys actually got.

Hall and Oates logic
(4 questions)

69. E. Since the other four answers aren't backed up in the passage, you have to go with the silly answer, (E), here. I'll have to stop with those now.

70. B. Hall's only hit was "Dreamtime" (#5), so it seems he wasn't much without Oates.

71. C. "Maneater" is catchy, but not the best song of all time. The best song of all time is "Girl You Know It's True" by Milli Vanilli.

72. D. This question pretty much answers #70 above, doesn't it?

Whose lead singer are you?
(15 questions)

Cheese rock

73. C. Reno was never seen without a headband.

74. E. His name sure wasn't "Tuff Enuff."

75. B. Zander was Cheap Trick's blond singer. Meanwhile, what was up with that guitarist?

76. D. Ann was the porky one.

77. A. The guy was geeky, but there's no denying the brilliance of "Don't Let Him Go."

Hard rock

78. B. Neil, too, had the "Looks That Kill," but in a different way.

79. A. Legions of people actually thought Michaels and drunken Poison guitarist C. C. DeVille were cool.

80. D. What the hell did Tawny Kitaen see in this loser?

81. E. Ratt's "Round and Round" still kicks ass.

82. C. Keifer had bad teeth.

Modern rock

83. D. Morrissey was the Pope of Mope ("Heaven Knows I'm Miserable Now," et al.).

84. E. New Order rose from the ashes of Joy Division, whose lead singer, Ian Curtis, hanged himself on May 18, 1980.

85. B. Among the many great tunes by Echo and the Bunnymen is "Lips Like Sugar."

86. C. Bauhaus did a great cover of Bowie's "Ziggy Stardust."

87. A. Smith looked pretty scary most of the time, but never more than in the "Why Can't I Be You?" video.

The video game
(25 questions)

88. B
89. B
90. D
91. B
92. B
93. B
94. D
95. B
96. C
97. A
98. B
99. A
100. E
101. A
102. D
103. C

104. C. "One" of the better videos of the decade: "It's Morse code. 'S.O.S.' — 'Help.'"
105. B. Waldo becomes a big mack-daddy pimp at the end.
106. A
107. D
108. C
109. B
110. E
111. E
112. D

Which doesn't fit?
(23 questions)

Big causes

113. D
114. A
115. A
116. B
117. D
118. B
119. E
120. D

121. C. Janet was still enjoying her stint on *Fame*.

122. B. It's hard to believe Sheila E. was there, especially without Prince, but she was.

Alternative music

123. B. Camper Van Beethoven did "Take the Skinheads Bowling."

124. E. "Everyday Is Like Sunday" is a Morrissey tune.

125. C. The dance club staple was called "Close to Me."

126. B. The Psychedelic Furs, or "the Furs" to those in the know, did "Love My Way."

127. E. "Who Needs Love Like That" was by Erasure.

128. D
129. E
130. B

Band members

131. **B.** The Edge's real name is *Dave* Evans.

132. **D.** It's *Jane* Wiedlin.

133. **E.** Michelle Irons . . . Michael Steele. You see the confusion.

134. **A.** Donnie Wahlberg was in NKOTB. Mark Wahlberg, aka Marky Mark, is his little brother.

135. **E.** Kendall Gill is a basketball player. Johnny Gill replaced Bobby Brown when he left.

Musical analogies

(30 questions)

Soundtracks

136. **A**
137. **B**
138. **A**
139. **A**
140. **B**
141. **A**
142. **C**
143. **B**
144. **E**
145. **D**

Albums

146. **E**
147. **C**
148. **D**
149. **D**

150. **E.** Did I mention that Sheena Easton was hot?

151. **C**
152. **B**
153. **B**
154. **E**
155. **A**

Foreigners

156. **C**

157. **E.** I won't say it again. (Okay, Sheena Easton was hot.)

158. **A**
159. **B**
160. **A**

Americans

161. D
162. E
163. D
164. B
165. C

Whose power ballad are you?
(10 questions)

Group 1

166. E
167. C
168. A
169. D
170. B

Group 2

171. D
172. E
173. A
174. C
175. B

Fill in the blanks
(25 questions)

Big-hair bands

176. E
177. D
178. A
179. B
180. C

One-hit wonders

181. E
182. A
183. D
184. E
185. E
186. D
187. B
188. A
189. B
190. C

Rap

191. C
192. D
193. C
194. A
195. C
196. B
197. E
198. B
199. C
200. A

Section IV — *Tube*

Theme song multiple choice
(25 questions)

1. **C**
2. **B**
3. **C.** Or was it "they got nothing but their jeans"? Or "genes"?
4. **E**
5. **D**
6. **E**
7. **B**
8. **E.** Crooned by Lee Majors himself.
9. **B**
10. **A**
11. **D**
12. **E**
13. **C**
14. **C**
15. **A**
16. **E**
17. **A**
18. **A**
19. **D**
20. **E**
21. **B**
22. **A**
23. **B**
24. **C.** "Don't be ridiculous, cousin."
25. **C**

What's my line?
(10 questions)

26. **D.** From *Diff'rent Strokes*
27. **B.** The furry houseguest is Alf.
28. **C.** From *Fantasy Island*
29. **A.** From *Hill Street Blues*
30. **D.** From *The A-Team*
31. **E.** *The Love Connection*
32. **E.** From *Moonlighting*
33. **A.** Doug Henning in the early '80s
34. **C.** From *The Dukes of Hazzard*
35. **A.** *The Incredible Hulk*

Saturday Night Live quote ID
(15 questions)

36. C. Crystal's Fernando character

37. D

38. E. From Hans and Franz

39. A. The Pathological Liar

40. B. Ed Grimley

41. D. Murphy as a convict-poet

42. A

43. E. The Church Lady

44. D. Mister Robinson

45. A. Master Thespian

46. D. Buckwheat

47. B. From the great *60 Minutes* parody

48. C. Tommy the Janitor

49. B. From the synchronized swimming sketch

50. E. Carvey's well-intentioned songwriter

Spin-off City
(10 questions)

51. E
52. A
53. C
54. D
55. B
56. A
57. D
58. B
59. D
60. C

Matching actors to their shows
(30 questions)

Bores

61. **D**
62. **E**
63. **A**
64. **C**
65. **B**

Boobs

66. **C**
67. **A**
68. **D**
69. **B**
70. **E**

Babes

71. **B**
72. **D**
73. **E**
74. **A**
75. **C**

Hunks

76. **A**
77. **D**
78. **C**
79. **E**
80. **B**

Geeks

81. **B**
82. **E**
83. **A**
84. **D**
85. **C**

Freaks

86. **E**
87. **C**
88. **B**
89. **A**
90. **D**

Tube analogies
(20 questions)

91. **B.** On *Remington Steele*, Zimbalist and Brosnan played private detectives between whom sparks flew, just like Dave and Maddie from *Moonlighting*.

92. **C.** On *Family Ties*, Skippy was Alex's neighbor, just like Bentley was to George Jefferson on *The Jeffersons*.

93. **B.** From *Newhart*, as in "Hi. I'm Larry. This is my brother Darryl and this is my other brother Darryl."

94. **A.** The key is to look for housekeepers, because that's what Mrs. Garrett was to Mr. Drummond on *Diff'rent Strokes*. Benson was a butler, Kate Summers (*Silver Spoons*) was Stratton's assistant, and Webster and Small Wonder just helped out around the house sometimes. Thus, it's Tony Micelli from *Who's the Boss?*

95. **C.** What is the correct role that follows from Pinchot's *Perfect Strangers* role? Only Beasley's *Moonlighting* gig.

96. **D.** Cockroach, like Boner, was a dumb but lovable best friend to the oldest son on their respective programs, *The Cosby Show* and *Growing Pains*.

97. **C.** Welles (*Magnum, P.I.*) is most like Forsythe (*Charlie's Angels*) because both of their characters were heard only over a speaker phone.

98. **C.** The two hosts' respective shows

99. **D.** Jock, like Blake, was the patriarch of his clan.

100. **E.** Both weren't the original hosts of their respective shows.

101. **A.** Hayley played Screech's teacher on *Saved by the Bell.*

102. **D.** If you don't remember Gary Gnu, what was your childhood like?

103. **A.** Llewelyn was Wapner's straitlaced sidekick, who always ended the show saying, "And remember: Don't take the law into your own hands. You take 'em to court."

104. **E.** We watched Doogie grow up at Eastman. Some of us did.

105. **B.** One of Chris Elliott's strange *Late Night with David Letterman* characters.

106. **B.** Big-haired Koppel hosted *Nightline;* overly serious Walsh hosted *AMW.*

107. **E.** Elvis was Crockett's pet alligator on *Miami Vice.*

108. **C.** Former football star Olsen played a man of the cloth in *Father Murphy.*

109. **D.** Like Somers's, Gerard's follow-up to his signature role (Buck Rogers) failed miserably.

110. **A.** Lt. Howard Hunter was one of the boys in blue in *Hill Street Blues.* Travanti was his captain, as Stewart was to Worf.

The Cosby Show story problem
(6 questions)

111. **D.** Sondra (played by Sabrina Le Beauf) almost never figured in any *Cosby Show* plots. What was wrong with her?

112. **A.** B'ooklyn's in da house! Da house is in B'ooklyn!

113. **D.** Noble profession, but I still wish Bill Cosby had stuck with *Fat Albert and the Cosby Kids* (like in answer C) for just a few more years. Hey, hey, hey!

114. **B.** His name was really Kenny, but Rudy insisted on calling him "Bud."

115. **C.** See *A Different World.*

116. **A.** Thursday has always been NBC's strong suit. At one point their lineup went *The Cosby Show, Family Ties, Cheers, Night Court,* and *Hill Street Blues.* Wow.

Dallas story problem

(6 questions)

117. D. Duh. This could be the easiest question on this test. (Sadly, *Dallas* never won the Emmy.)

118. C. *Knots Landing* lasted from 1979 to 1993, longer than *Dallas* itself (1978–91).

119. A. Boy, that was good television.

120. C. On the other side of the TV coin was the Dream Season. At the end of the 1984–85 season, Bobby Ewing (Patrick Duffy) was killed in a hit-and-run accident. The entire 1985–86 season went on without him. The following year, though, Duffy came back to the fold, and they wrote off his death — and the entire previous season — as a dream imagined by Pam Ewing (Victoria Principal).

121. E. Charlene Tilton played Lucy, the daughter of Gary, who was the black sheep of the Ewing clan. Gary was the brother of J.R.; therefore, Lucy was J.R.'s niece.

122. B. From the letter, you don't know if Larry Hagman has won an Emmy (although he hasn't) or if he's got the hots for Tilton (in III), but you do know he wants that Outstanding Drama Emmy. That was pretty easy.

Which does not fit?

(15 questions)

123. B. Captain Lou Albano was Cyndi Lauper's professional wrestling cohort.

124. B
125. B
126. D
127. C

128. A. *Seinfeld*'s Michael Richards was on another sketch comedy show, *Fridays* (1980–82), but no one ever watched that.

129. A
130. E

131. A. Bear was the the pet chimp of the self-titled *B.J. and the Bear*. (Ubu was the dog that was told to sit after every episode of *Family Ties*.)

132. D. She was widowed.

133. E. They never do too well, do they?

134. C. It was *Shōgun*, of course.

135. B. It didn't serve coffee, either.

136. D. *Dear John* (C) had Judd Hirsch (*Taxi*'s Alex), *Who's the Boss?* (E) had Tony Danza (Tony in both series), and *Wizards and Warriors* (B) starred Jeff Conaway (Bobby). *Taxi* (A) starred all of 'em. Yep.

137. E. St. Eligius was in Boston.

Premise descriptions

(25 questions)

138. E. What was Mr. Belvedere's first name? Lynn. I knew there was something wrong with that guy.

139. B. Dabney Coleman has long been involved with TV failures, starring in five shows that didn't last longer than a season — *The Slap Maxwell Story, Buffalo Bill, Apple Pie, Drexell's Class,* and *Madman of the People.* He would rival Hector Elizondo for futility, except for his successful movie career, which includes great roles in *WarGames, Cloak & Dagger, Tootsie,* and *9 to 5,* among others.

140. B. Other guest stars who appeared on *Amazing Stories:* Mark Hamill, Drew Barrymore, Milton Berle, and Charlie Sheen. Among the guest directors: Burt Reynolds, Clint Eastwood, Martin Scorsese, and Spielberg himself. Good show!

141. A. When Bogg (played by future prop-gun victim Jon-Erik Hexum) and the snot-nosed Jeffrey Jones (Meeno Peluce, Punky Brewster's brother) activated the Omni, they would seemingly fly through space and then fall, with a thud, in the middle of some historical event. They didn't know how to work the Omni, because they lost the manual, just like the Greatest American Hero did with the instructions for his suit.

142. C. Scott Baio was indeed in charge. Do you remember when he set the record in the obstacle course in one of those *Battle of the Network Stars* competitions? (If this show were around today, it might well be called *Charles — You Da Man!*)

143. C. And don't ever forget about Skip Stephenson.

144. B. *The Tracey Ullman Show,* like *Married ... With Children* and *21 Jump Street,* was on Fox's first schedule when it debuted in 1987.

145. D. Those little whammies were so cute, but, man, they were evil little devils.

146. D. Three more words: Bonnie was hot.

147. C. It really is amazing that Clooney has starred in two shows named *ER.*

148. E. *Automan* was the TV version of *Tron,* without the video game tie-in or the good acting.

149. B. What a show *Silver Spoons* was. In addition to featuring the talents of Jason Bateman (as snively Derek Taylor), there were a few notable guest stars, including Menudo, Whitney Houston (as a flame of straitlaced lawyer Dexter Stuffins), and Gary Coleman. But the main reason to watch: Erin Gray. Hello!

150. D. It was not Weathers's good fortune to appear in this show and then go straight to *Action Jackson.*

151. E. Bakula then made a quantum, uh, hop over to *Eisenhower & Lutz,* a sitcom costarring *Home Improvement*'s Patricia Richardson. It tanked, too.

152. B. Well, isn't that special.

153. A. *The Master* was almost as bad as *Kung Fu: The Legend Continues.*

154. B. *Spencer* (please don't confuse it with *Spenser: For Hire*) failed in part because Chad Lowe wanted more money and left the show after only a few episodes.

155. B. The guy from *Electric Company* was Joe Santos. Morgan Freeman was also on *The Electric Company,* as the Easy Reader ("Be cool. Read a book.").

156. C. The cool unlikely-superhero show starred Robert Culp (who appeared in *Turk 182!*), Connie Sellecca (as "Counseler"), and William Katt, who never learned how to fly.

157. D. She played the niece of Henry Rush (Ted Knight) and, thankfully, was only on for a year.

158. A. When *Diff'rent Strokes* brought on country-crooning Danny Cooksey in 1984 because Gary Coleman's chubby-cheeked cuteness had all but vanished, the show really began to suck bad.

159. D. Question: What ever happened to Joel Higgins (who later played Mr. Stratton on *Silver Spoons*)?

160. E. These teenage sleuths employed a pin-hole camera in one classic case. They solved, you learned.

161. A. Ted McGinley gets no respect. Although he's never around when a show is just getting popular (see *Happy Days, The Love Boat, Married . . . with Children, Dynasty*), he's always game when he gets there.

162. B. Unfortunately for the annoying performing arts students on this show, their fame didn't last forever, with the exception of Janet Jackson and, arguably, Lori Singer.

Daytime TV
(15 questions)

163.	**B**
164.	**A**
165.	**C**
166.	**B**
167.	**E**
168.	**B**
169.	**E**
170.	**C**
171.	**B**
172.	**D**
173.	**C**
174.	**E**
175.	**B**
176.	**C**
177.	**B**

Fill in the blanks
(23 questions)

Annoying Saturday-morning TV characters

178.	**D**
179.	**B**
180.	**B**
181.	**A**
182.	**C**
183.	**E**

Aaron Spelling shows

184.	**C**
185.	**A**
186.	**E**
187.	**B**
188.	**D**
189.	**B**
190.	**A**
191.	**E**
192.	**C**

TV commercials

193.	**A**
194.	**B**
195.	**D**
196.	**E**
197.	**B**
198.	**D**
199.	**C**
200.	**E**

Before figuring your total PCAT rating, you need to see how you did on the warm-up Rad '80s section. After grading Section I using the answer key on pages 137–140, take the number of questions you got correct and refer to the following chart to find out if you're ready for the rest of the PCAT.

Section I — *The Rad '80s*

If you scored . . .   *then . . .*

70–80	Dude, you're stoked! Fuckin' A!
60–69	You're on the '80s jazz, man.
55–59	If only you could make money with this stuff.
50–54	The '80s are over. Move on, dude.
45–49	You've hung out in a mall or two in your day.
40–44	You're no stranger to all things Rubik, but put down the *USA Today*.
30–39	Nerd alert! Your nickname was the Geek, right?
20–29	Gross-o-rama! Take off, hoser.
10–19	I pity the fool who does worse than you!
0–9	Did you, like, live in a cave during the '80s?

Like the SAT, your overall PCAT score is what really matters. After grading Sections II–IV using the answer key on pages 141–162, take the number of questions you got correct in each section and refer to the chart below to find your scaled score for that section. (Note: It's a little complicated, but that's why you don't get your scores for eight weeks.)

Raw Score	Scaled Score
180–200	800
176–179	790
173–175	780
170–172	770
167–169	760
164–166	750
161–163	740
159–160	730
157–158	720
155–156	710
152–154	700
148–151	690
145–147	680
142–144	670
139–141	660
136–138	650
133–135	640
130–132	630
127–129	620
125–126	610
123–124	600

Raw Score	Scaled Score		Raw Score	Scaled Score
120–122	590		60–62	390
118–119	580		57–59	380
115–117	570		54–56	370
112–114	560		51–53	360
110–111	550		48–50	350
107–109	540		45–47	340
104–106	530		42–44	330
101–103	520		39–41	320
98–100	510		36–38	310
95–97	500		34–35	300
92–94	490		32–33	290
89–91	480		30–31	280
85–88	470		28–29	270
82–84	460		26–27	260
79–81	450		24–25	250
75–78	440		22–23	240
72–74	430		20–21	230
69–71	420		18–19	220
66–68	410		16–17	210
63–65	400		0–15	200

Total Score

Now add the scaled scores from Sections II, III, and IV.
Take a deep breath and then refer to the following chart to find out your
final '80s PCAT ranking.

GO ON TO THE NEXT PAGE →